Farrow&Ball®
HOW TO DECORATE

JOA STUDHOLME & CHARLOTTE COSBY

MITCHELL BEAZLEY

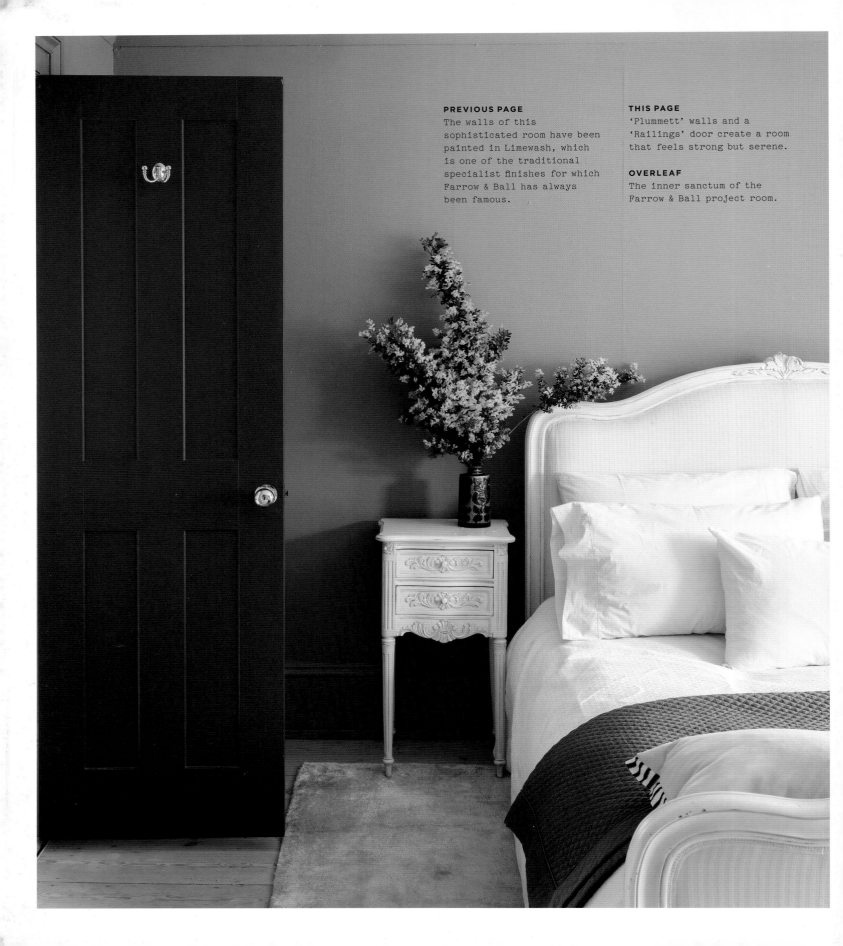

PREVIOUS PAGE
The walls of this sophisticated room have been painted in Limewash, which is one of the traditional specialist finishes for which Farrow & Ball has always been famous.

THIS PAGE
'Plummett' walls and a 'Railings' door create a room that feels strong but serene.

OVERLEAF
The inner sanctum of the Farrow & Ball project room.

INTRODUCTION

Farrow & Ball has defined the colour choices of a generation, and what better thing can there be than to bring colour into people's lives?

Choosing a colour or a wallpaper should be an adventure as well as a journey of self-discovery. However, this book is not so much about your choice of colour as about how to use it and understand its effect. It is reassuring, but possibly a little daunting, to know that there are no strict rules when it comes to decorating, so the following ideas are here not so much to influence but to inspire, and to help you bring your vision to life.

Farrow & Ball colours have stood the test of time in a diversity of domestic environments. They have been used in the restoration of historic interiors as well as being enjoyed by contemporary interior designers and homeowners. Each colour is meticulously researched and reflects the company's unique heritage. The Farrow & Ball range is a fabulous encyclopedia of past colours and patterns, rediscovered and reinvigorated for a modern audience.

Colour and pattern are one of the greatest forms of self-expression and the possibilities are myriad, so Farrow & Ball offers a thoughtfully created palette of 132 colours to help you with your choice. If you want to use colour to make a statement, then the basic ways in which the red, yellow, blue, green and dark families are effective in decorating are covered in this book. Should you want the colours of your home to be historically accurate, there is a broad outline of the colours used in four main decorative periods. If you would prefer to use the famous Farrow & Ball neutral families, they too are covered, together with suggestions on how to use them to create the most subtle and sophisticated of rooms.

The book includes detailed advice on how to approach every architectural element in the home, including the thorny subjects of ceiling colour and how to make the most of the natural light in your rooms. Using colour is all about combination, so the three basic ways of combining colours are comprehensively explored, as

is the use of colour on floors. There are also some suggestions for decorating the rooms of the younger members of the household.

The homes included in this book are varied, chosen, in part, to demonstrate particular decorating methods, as well as to showcase individual and divergent styles. Wherever they are in the world, they are all owned by people who have come back to Farrow & Ball time and time again, taking comfort in returning to a trusted friend. Colour is a matter of personal preference and our home is where we can be true to ourselves, so the colour choices reflect the personalities and the stories of each household.

Different periods, styles and tastes are all covered here. Some schemes have an understated approach, with rooms that are calm and restrained but still have a depth and richness, while others are a kaleidoscope of brilliantly contrasting colours. Colour offers almost infinite possibilities, and the same hue that appears fun to one person can be garish to another. Beauty is certainly in the eye of the beholder.

The wonderful resonant names of the Farrow & Ball range still give the not entirely inaccurate picture that they, and also the colours, are invented around a kitchen table. Some of the inspiration behind the creation of these names and the colours themselves are shared in this book.

Although founded 70 years ago, Farrow & Ball only opened its first showroom in London in 1996, when I was lucky enough to join the company. I had no formal training. I am Farrow & Ball home-grown, nurtured by an astonishing group of people. However, as a child, I did spend an inordinate amount of time rearranging my set of Caran d'Ache crayons to see how different colour combinations worked. My dolls' house was constantly redecorated and I was always experimenting with colour, painting my ceiling bright yellow to try to fill the room with sunlight or creating cosy spaces in cupboards by painting them dark. I was already a half-formed colour geek and couldn't wait to explore its visual magic.

FACING PAGE
'Shaded White' walls and an
'All White' ceiling — what
more do you need?

BELOW
Stunning 'Chinese Blue' (A)
flatters antique furniture
and portraits to perfection.

I have been lucky enough to work with the phenomenon that is Farrow & Ball for the past 19 years, helping to develop and name new colours, as well as looking at colour trends. An enormous amount of my time is taken up working in my role as a colour consultant, helping people in their own homes to choose their paint colours and decide how to combine them.

This role has taken me all over the world – to castles on the shores of lakes, to churches, to private members clubs and to a smattering of homes belonging to music and film stars. One thing I have learned is that it is just as exciting and challenging to be decorating a diminutive basement property as it is a palace, and that the same basic principles apply to both. It is these principles that form the backbone of this book.

In 2007, an exuberant bundle of energy in the shape of Charlotte Cosby arrived at Farrow & Ball, and she has expertly aided me in producing this book. Charlotte is now Head of Creative and her enthusiasm for colour and pattern, like mine, knows no bounds. We have worked happily together to share with you some secrets about the intriguing world of Farrow & Ball, as well as the myriad ways you can change your home with our paints and papers.

Included are some indispensable practical tools in the form of decorating tips and some fail-safe Farrow & Ball colour combinations. Our intention is that you can use this book as a manual to refer to when you have a decorating quandary but also when you simply need some inspiration. Hopefully, it will help to turn your ideas and dreams into reality.

Watching paint dry may be a familiar metaphor for tedium, but I cannot think of a better way to spend time – excitedly anticipating the final colour that will enhance our homes and enrich our lives.

The Victorian art critic John Ruskin wrote that 'The purest and most thoughtful minds are those which love colour the most.' At Farrow & Ball, we certainly agree.

— *Joa Studholme*

THE FARROW & BALL STORY

Farrow & Ball has deep roots. The company was founded in 1946 by John Farrow, an industrial chemist, and Richard Ball, an engineer, who had recently returned from Germany where he had been a prisoner of war. Fortuitously, the two met when they both worked at a clay pit and they later went on to establish their first paint factory together in Verwood, Dorset. Their reputation for quality quickly spread until the pair were asked to supply paint to the Admiralty and the War Office.

In the 1960s, Farrow & Ball moved to its current site on Uddens Estate, near Wimborne, and continued to expand successfully throughout the 1970s and '80s. But while other paint manufacturers started to create acrylic paints containing more plastic and less pigment, Farrow & Ball continued using its original formulations, the finest ingredients, rich pigments and traditional processes, to make really high-quality paint that was quite different from that of the commercial brands. This was all done out of the limelight in the heart of sleepy Dorset, which helped the company retain its identity and heritage, both of which would prove to be important factors in making the company so successful in the years to come.

In the early 1990s, historical decorator Tom Helme was commissioned to develop a range of paints for the National Trust, but he was unable to find a producer who could match his exacting standards, until he came across the then sleepy Farrow & Ball. He was joined by his school friend, corporate financier Martin Ephson, and together they took over the running of the company.

FACING PAGE
A very old and much-treasured original Farrow & Ball paint tin. We still make our paint in Dorset to this day.

The National Trust paints were born by working closely with historical buildings and creating colours that were sympathetic to their era. Suddenly the dedicated trade-based customers, who were the company's usual clients, were joined by an army of people interested in interior design, all of whom were desperate to purchase paints that they could see had a different look: an unsurpassed depth of colour. The names and colours were now being talked about in revered tones all over the UK, and in 1996 the first Farrow & Ball flagship showroom opened on Fulham Road in Chelsea, London, followed in 1999 by the first overseas showroom in Toronto, Canada.

Over the following years, Farrow & Ball continued to grow apace, opening showrooms in Europe and North America, along with an ever-expanding number in the UK. The showrooms were styled more like a library or a museum than a typical paint store and they soon became a magnet for people wishing to peruse the now world-famous palette of 132 paint colours, as well as the handcrafted wallpapers, in a spacious, peaceful environment. Every colour we have ever made is still available from our archive. Archive colours are marked with an (A) in this book.

Farrow & Ball has certainly put its stamp on the world of interiors and home decor globally, while sticking to its roots and remaining true to its craft. Every batch of paint and roll of wallpaper is still made with the utmost care and meticulously checked in its Dorset factory.

Today, Farrow & Ball distributes its unsurpassed paints and artisanal papers to 67 countries worldwide and has more than 50 showrooms, where you can work out your dreams in colour. It is no longer a sleepy little Dorset company.

COLOUR NAMES & INSPIRATION

Sometime in the early 1990s there began a whole new topic of conversation at many dinner parties. People were chatting regularly about the richness of 'Mouse's Back' or the scrumptious 'Smoked Trout', along with the delicacy of 'Pea Green' (A). It became quickly evident that this was not the contents of a Bacchanalian feast but the names of a palette of paints that had suddenly taken the world by storm. The names were so intriguing that one's imagination ran wild trying to visualize the colour with which they were associated. This was the first time I fell under the Farrow & Ball spell. The names are now iconic and although the concept has been much copied, uniquely each and every one of our names has meaning. They are meticulously researched and reflect our individual heritage.

We are more than aware that the psychology of colour names is powerful. Many people might doubt the wisdom of calling a colour 'Dead Salmon', for example, but this name is actually derived from a painting bill found for the decorating of the library at Kedleston Hall, Derbyshire, in 1805. Salmon is the colour and Dead actually refers to the matt paint finish rather than a deceased fish. There are many other names that emanate from the animal kingdom, ranging from the delicate tone of 'Cabbage White', named after the equally delicate butterfly, to the more robust if vaporous 'Elephant's Breath' and 'Mole's Breath' – two of the most-discussed Farrow & Ball names. However, all the names are rooted in much more than quirkiness or attention-seeking. We use the connotative power of language to describe colours. 'Setting Plaster' is named after the blushing walls of newly plastered houses, a colour that we have all been tempted not to cover. 'String' is, of course, the colour of untreated twine and works in perfect combination with 'Cord', another type of twine. These colour and name associations are intentional, if a little esoteric. 'Ammonite' was so named after the beautiful fossils found on the Isle of Purbeck, Dorset, and so sits naturally with 'Purbeck Stone'.

As true colourists, we at Farrow & Ball often take inspiration from original pigments, sometimes with surprising consequences. 'India Yellow' is famously named after the pigment collected from the urine of cows that had been given a special diet of mango leaves. The rather grim-sounding 'Arsenic' makes reference to the pigment that, historically, was often used in green wallpapers – there is a theory that Napoleon 1 may have been poisoned by the arsenic used in the decoration of his bathroom in St Helena where he was held in exile. But please let me reassure you that there is nothing poisonous in these paints today.

Occasionally, the paint name comes almost before the colour. 'Plummett' was mixed after an afternoon spent fishing on the river, where the colour of the lead used to weight the fisherman's line was a thing of such beauty that it just begged to be added to the Farrow & Ball palette.

Similarly, there was a deep desire to make a white that was almost gossamer in appearance – a white with very little additional colour and almost translucent – like a spider's web. This was the birth of the colour 'Wevet', named after the Dorset dialect for exactly that: a spider's web.

Because Farrow & Ball has its roots firmly in the county of Dorset, England, other paint names have been taken from the local dialect. Although not recognizable words, they are somehow so evocative that they bring the colour to mind anyway. We all know the hue of a mix of mist and drizzle, which creates the colour 'Mizzle'. 'Dimpse' is also quaint local dialect for the colour of the sky, but this time at twilight.

These colours are joined by another weather-related name, 'Cromarty', a sea area referred to in the BBC radio broadcast of the Shipping Forecast, which warns sailors about impending gales and is very much part of the fabric of British life. 'Cromarty', a little lighter than 'Mizzle', conjures up the colours of swirling mists and turbulent seas.

THIS PAGE
The beginning of the lengthy
process of mixing new
colours. Fairly basic, using
the eye and a teaspoon, but
still extremely effective.

Many of the Farrow & Ball colours have taken their cue from historic houses. 'Picture Gallery Red' was inspired by the picture gallery at Attingham Park, Shropshire, while 'Sudbury Yellow' is an interpretation of John Fowler's wall colour for the staircase at Sudbury Hall, Derbyshire. 'Calke Green' is based on a cleaned version of the colour found in the breakfast room at Calke Abbey, also in Derbyshire. 'Cook's Blue' was also inspired there, by the walls in the cook's closet, which have remained untouched over many decades. It is said that the colour was used to deter flies.

The tradition of looking to historic houses to find colours endures to this day. Many that we create are based on surviving paintwork or on traditional colours handed down by successive generations of painters. In 2012, while working on the magnificent St Giles House, the Dorset home of Lord Shaftesbury, we came across some ancient wallpaper that had been used in the hall. From that small scrap, 'St Giles Blue' was born – a colour that feels clean and contemporary, even though it was was sourced from a house that had its first stone laid in the 15th century. Similarly, 'Inchyra Blue' was inspired by a bespoke colour created for Lord and Lady Inchyra for their classic Georgian Inchyra House in Perthshire. The colour needed to be sympathetic to the house's dramatic backdrop and work with the moody Scottish skies.

COLOUR NAMES & INSPIRATION

ABOVE
The uncertain colour of
the sky when there is a mix
of mist and drizzle is the
inspiration for the paint
colour 'Mizzle'.

FACING PAGE
The faces behind the
names, clockwise from top
left: Nancy of 'Nancy's
Blushes'; Joa of 'Joa's
White'; and Charlotte of
'Charlotte's Locks'.

Other Farrow & Ball colours also started as bespoke shades. 'Print Room Yellow' (A) was mixed specially for the early restoration of an 18th-century print room, and delicate 'James White', with its underlying green, was created for the garden room of discerning Dr James, one of our first ever colour consultancy clients.

Nature, however, will always be the greatest inspiration. 'Calluna', for example, is the colour, as well as the name, of the beautiful heather that brings late summer to life in the most rugged landscapes, while its stronger counterpart 'Brassica' was inspired by the colour of the leaves of purple sprouting broccoli.

Sometimes a colour is made because it comes to light that there is something of a gap in the colour card. The amusingly named 'Vert De Terre', which is indeed close to the blue-green of the verditer pigment, was created as an alternative to both 'Cooking Apple Green' and 'Ball Green', with the former being somewhat fresher and the latter more subtle and muted. 'Vert De Terre' is the perfect alternative that lies between the two.

We certainly hope to lead colour trends rather than follow them; when both 'Pavilion Gray' and 'Manor House Gray' were created, it was just before the current grey mania. Although they are perfect in the cutting-edge contemporary home, they were both inspired by the colours of ancient buildings: one a cricket pavilion, the other a historic boarding house in a famous college for boys.

The inspirations behind these colours are numerous – how lucky we are to live in a world so full of glorious colour.

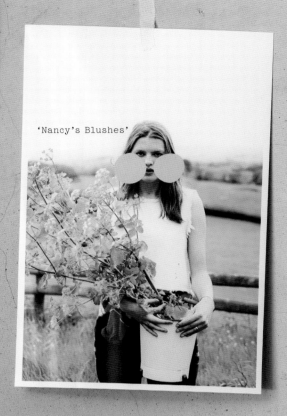

'Nancy's Blushes'

'Joa's White'

'Charlotte's Locks'

A deserving lucky few have had colours named after them. 'Ball Green' is a tribute to Richard Ball, the paint pioneer who first founded the company along with John Farrow, after whom 'Farrow's Cream' is named. 'Savage Ground' owes its name to Dennis Savage, a block printer *par excellence*, who was instrumental in the creation of our very first wallpapers, while 'Cornforth White' was named in memory of John Cornforth, the revered architectural historian and co-author of *English Decoration in the 18th Century*. More recently, colours have been named after members of the creative team in a light-hearted appreciation of their contribution to the colour palette.

The paint names are now as much a part of our colours as the shades themselves. They bring the colours to life and are inspired by myriad surprising sources. Who would have guessed that 'Stiffkey Blue' is named after the mud on a particular beach on the north Norfolk coast? But they are also sourced from the downright familiar: 'Brinjal', whose sumptuous tone is difficult to resist, is taken from the Indian name for the glossy aubergine, or eggplant.

CREATING PAINT & PAPER

There is a kind of alchemy that takes place during the creation of our paints, and that is why they look different. However, they often start life in the simplest of ways, usually at a kitchen table. Tens of ramekins filled with different shades are mixed and remixed for weeks on end until we are happy with the exact colour. They are then sent to the paint experts in our laboratory to be tested again.

Although we now make paint appropriate for every surface, Farrow & Ball was known originally for its specialist finishes, such as Dead Flat and Casein Distemper. Much was learned from the traditional production of these paints, which had very high levels of pigmentation, and now every finish from Farrow & Ball, ranging from Estate Emulsion to Full Gloss, has those same high levels of pigment, along with rich resin binders combined to create our signature depth of colour. The complex pigmentation produces uniquely interesting colours that have redolence and depth in their undertones. This causes them to change subtly in different light conditions, making the colours feel magical and alive. The high refractory nature of all the key ingredients produces a softer, flatter finish than many other commercial brands.

Some people question the fact that Farrow & Ball paint is not thick, that it has the texture of single, or light, cream, rather than the jelly-like texture of cheaper commercial paints. This is because it is packed with lots of rich pigment rather than plastic binders. The less viscous nature of the paint also ensures that it flows well, to create an even surface. Every colour is blended with enormous care and precision and is scrupulously tested before it even reaches the tin, because we believe that paint is more than just a veneer.

The same care and precision is put into practice when making wallpaper. Throughout history, block-printed papers have always been treasured, but recently most of the work produced via this method has been purely for the restoration of historic houses. Although the technique used at Farrow & Ball for making wallpaper was first developed in the 18th century, the company has fortunately also benefited from technology available in the 21st.

Each wallpaper design is achieved using a hand-brushing technique to apply the background colour, which results in visible brushstrokes, just as it would have done in the 18th century. The blocks for the patterns have Farrow & Ball colour applied to them and are then overlaid onto the paper. The use of our own paint not only increases the depth of colour and makes each part of the pattern stand slightly proud, but it also imparts a pleasing tactility that cannot be emulated by printer's ink. Colour that is printed on top of colour produces remarkable effects that are impossible to achieve by any other means. There are slight variations from one repeat to the next, making the papers feel even more handcrafted.

The French damask 'St Antoine' and its English counterpart 'Silvergate' were the first damasks to be produced by this traditional block-printing method for decades. They have since been joined by many pretty botanic florals, as well as some more contemporary geometric patterns, all of which have been inspired by archives of evocative papers and fabrics from around the world.

Farrow & Ball has always been famous for its traditional stripes and drags, which are produced using the open-trough method. Paper is brush-painted with a ground colour that will form the background. Once dry, this roll of ground paper is passed slowly under paint-filled, open-bottom troughs. To create our stripes, foam pads are hand-cut into each of our striped designs before the trough is divided, allowing the chosen paint colour to flow steadily onto the pads beneath.

FACING PAGE
Our dedicated and loyal staff in the factory take enormous pride in the paint they produce and constantly check its quality and colour.

OVERLEAF
The wallpaper factory is full of exciting treasures, from the rolls of ground paper to the meticulously made blocks and rollers.

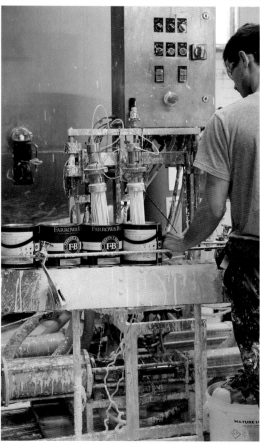

PART ONE

—

WHERE TO START

FACING PAGE
The joy of 'All White', used
on the walls of this kitchen,
is that it contains no
pigment other than white.
This gives an unsurpassed
softness and none of the
uncomfortable qualities of
a brilliant white.

INTERIOR ARCHITECTURAL DETAIL

Ceiling

Coving

Glazing Bars

Wall

Window Frame/Architrave

Dado Rail/Chair Rail

Panelling/Dado

Skirting/Baseboard

Floor

INTERIOR ARCHITECTURAL DETAIL

Ceiling Rose

Ceiling

Cornice/Crown Moulding

Frieze

Picture Rail

Wall

Doorframe/Architrave

Dado Rail/Chair Rail

Door

Dado

Skirting/Baseboard

Floor

EXTERIOR ARCHITECTURAL DETAIL

Ridge Tiles

Roof

Chimney Stack

Fascia Boards

Barge Board

Quoin

Windows & Frame

Corbel

Front Door & Frame

Plinth

INSPIRATION

———

Scrapbooks are often associated with childhood memories of vacations spent collecting all sorts of wonderful treasures. However, they can also be an excellent record of your home's history and how it was decorated, as well as an invaluable aid for future plans. A collection of ideas and inspirations laid out with care on each page can help to clarify decisions and shape your approach to decorating your home.

To start your inspirations book, collect images of anything with a colour or combination of colours that you love – these don't have to match, they just need to work together. We are surrounded by colour in our daily lives, from nature to advertising billboards. Let your instincts lead you; consider the colours you like to wear, as they are your most obvious form of self-expression.

The colours of nature are always inspiring and an obvious starting point. We can learn so much from nature, where colours harmonize and work naturally together.

Take pictures of anything in a colour that appeals, such as a front door that catches your eye or a summer sky. Gather together objects of particular beauty – the iconic colours of Hermès and Tiffany packaging have been the inspiration for many a decorating scheme. Look at websites such as Houzz and Pinterest, as well as art and design books or magazines.

FACING PAGE
This carefully gathered box of treasures is a wonderful starting point for deciding which colours you want to live with. Who would believe that a whole decorative scheme could evolve from the palest of threads, some tree bark, a shoe or even the colour of a wooden mouse?

THIS PAGE
All the wood cladding and trim in this recently built houseboat belonging to photographer James Merrell is painted in 'Cornforth White', one of the Easy Neutrals (see page 88).

This helps to minimize any distraction from the houseboat's beautiful shape and allows ultimate connection with the surrounding water, which is a similar tone to 'Cornforth White'.

The smallest of items within your home can be the deciding factor – entire decorating schemes can be built around a single cushion or piece of tableware. If you choose to use existing furniture or curtains in your new scheme, include images or fabric swatches of those in your scrapbook too.

Historic houses can also provide valuable reference, however humble your own home may be. The work of great designers, such as Robert Adam, who used striking mixed schemes comprising as many as six colours on one ceiling, or John Fowler, probably the greatest colourist of his generation, can be wonderfully inspirational.

Art, too, can be a great influence, whether you are drawn to the thrilling mix of colours used in Mark Rothko's abstract work or the muted neutral tones of Giorgio Morandi's still lifes. Your wall colour needs to enhance any work of art you have on display, so make sure they work well together.

Exotic palettes gathered from your travels are also a rich source of inspiration, but you should be wary of them appearing garish when used in different light. The exotic hue of a dazzling sari may well appear lurid when removed from bright sunshine, so consider using such bold colours as accents against a neutral background. Vibrant colours demand your attention and require an artful balance when used in the home.

Whatever your inspiration, it is best to gather as many elements together as you can, including all floor covering, tiles and fabrics. Look at how they react to each other – some colours will recede while others demand your attention, so you may need to rework the mix. Treat them as ingredients for your own personal home recipe, each one as delicious and important as the other. As long as you let your instincts guide you, you will be all set to embark on your decorating adventure.

ABOVE RIGHT
A summer vacation photograph and a shell found while beachcombing are the obvious inspiration behind choosing a scheme of 'Green Blue', 'Red Earth' and 'Off-White'.

RIGHT
Fabrics, rugs and even tableware are often a great starting point for a decorative scheme. Here, 'Calke Green' is proposed for the walls, to sit perfectly with the curtain fabric, while a dresser will be painted in 'Stiffkey Blue' with a 'Charlotte's Locks' interior, to make the very most of the display of decorative plates.

3 THINGS TO THINK ABOUT

ARCHITECTURE, LIGHT & STYLE

There are no hard-and-fast rules when it comes to decorating. Luckily, we all gravitate to different styles, live in different places and like different colours – the world would be a much duller place if this were not the case. However, it is certainly helpful to bear the following three pointers in mind when starting to decorate:

The architectural elements of the room
The light
Your style

Every room is different, so the choice of colour should be influenced by the particular conditions of the space: how it functions, its architecture and when it is used.

FACING PAGE
Sometimes the simplest designs are the most effective and monochrome schemes, such as this, have an enduring appeal. 'Wevet' on the walls and the very slightly darker 'Strong White' on the woodwork create the perfect backdrop for the elegant black table and chair.

ARCHITECTURE

—

SIZE AND SHAPE

Colour can appear to visually alter the proportions of a room, changing its size and shape. Lighter colours are often best suited to big rooms because they maximize the space and won't feel overpowering. In contrast, darker tones will enhance small areas and make them feel more intimate.

To make a bold statement in a large room can be daunting. Tiny spaces, on the other hand, can be treated like jewel boxes. Pack them with fabulous colour, rather than leaving them drab and colourless. Strong colours soften a room and are the perfect distraction, making you focus on how stylish the room is, rather than its size. If your room is an awkward shape, with crushingly low or looming high ceilings, these problems can be solved by the simple use of colour as outlined in the following chapters.

RIGHT
The owners of this West London apartment have been incredibly bold in their use of colour. Every door and window frame has been made to look larger with a very wide border painted in classic 'Railings'. In the sitting room, this dramatic colour has been combined with smouldering 'Green Smoke', proving that it is often more effective to use strong colours in small spaces.

FACING PAGE
The original brick wall of this chic French home can be glimpsed behind the reclaimed glazed doors of the kitchen cupboards. This not only reminds us of the integrity of the building, but also adds an interesting layer of texture. 'Black Blue' has been used on the cupboard surround to make the doors stand out against the 'Manor House Gray' walls.

The walls and ceiling in this charming Dorset cottage have been painted in 'Cromarty', the perfect soft blue-grey to fade into the background and look as if it has always been there. Using the equally soft but more coloured 'Pigeon' on all the woodwork draws the eye to the idiosyncrasies of the room.

RIGHT

In the dressing area of a painstakingly renovated Georgian house in Bath, the cupboard doors have been beautifully disguised by painting them the same colour as the panelled wall. Rich 'Claydon Blue' (A) has been used to draw the eye into this intriguing space from the bedroom, which is painted in a neutral 'Strong White'.

OVERLEAF

There can rarely be a stronger architectural statement than this extraordinary cantilever staircase. The tall kitchen units and facing wall, which are painted in 'Off-Black', sit perfectly with the steel support, while the stairs themselves tally with the 'All White' end wall and the island, creating a perfectly balanced scheme — a remarkable feat when incorporating such an amazingly bold feature.

DETAIL

It is important to familiarize yourself with all the architectural features of your room and its peculiarities before starting to paint (see also pages 155 and 163). Small tonal changes usually enhance architectural features, and quieter palettes will make the most of small spaces – the more contrasts there are, the less relaxed and smaller a room feels. Or perhaps you would prefer to paint every element in the room the same. Rooms in one colour, no matter how rich, are restful and tend to draw the eye away from mundane features such as picture rails, chair rails and architraves. If you use just one colour in a room, on both the walls and the woodwork, this can afford to be fairly dark, as strong tones recede, creating an illusion of space when not used in contrast with lighter colours.

LIGHT

hether the room you are decorating benefits from bright southern sunshine or indirect northern light (if you are based in the northern hemisphere and vice versa if you are in the southern hemisphere), the most important thing is to monitor how its appearance changes throughout the day. You will then better understand the effect that light and shade have on colour.

Without light there is no colour, and the joy of the heavily pigmented Farrow & Ball paints is how they react to different light conditions. Their colour changes through the course of the day, which makes them feel alive and exciting. In the morning the light is bluer, at midday it is fairly neutral, while evening light is somewhat warmer. Due to the highly complex nature of their pigment, even the Neutrals (see pages 78–91), with their different undertones, react subtly to changing light conditions.

It is always tempting to use light colours in small, dark spaces, but this generally results in a dull, visually unappetizing room. Although a strong colour in such a space might seem counterintuitive, the results can be wonderfully theatrical and much more exciting than any attempt made to create light by painting a room white.

Interconnecting rooms can benefit from a subtle, tone-on-tone approach and using colours that have equal strength is particularly harmonious. However, an entrance hall, especially one with little or no natural light, that is painted a dark colour exudes glamour at the point of arrival and means that every room leading off it feels bigger and brighter. Conversely, large, light rooms are best suited to lighter tones of paint, which then lead to glimpses of intriguing darker colour in smaller adjacent rooms.

FACING PAGE

The underlying green in 'Mouse's Back' makes it the perfect colour to use upstairs in this Toronto home. The colour in the room is totally sympathetic with the view, so the tree, which is often bathed in light, remains the star. However, as the light fades, the colour on the panelling will feel stronger, creating a more cocoon-like space.

THIS PAGE

The simplicity of this space makes it so appealing for sitting in and working. No artwork is required on this expansive wall, which is painted in 'Cornforth White', because the extraordinary top light creates shadows of rare beauty. These, together with the paint colour, will change and excite throughout the course of the day.

FACING PAGE

Few rooms are filled with such enormous amounts of natural light as this Parisian example. The light, which comes from two sources — the windows and the skylight — creates endless excitement on the walls. This means that the room requires no more colour than 'Ammonite', with an accent of 'Railings' on the fire surround. At night, small pools of light are created by the use of mismatched floor lamps.

BELOW LEFT

The owners of this striking West Country farmhouse have been extremely bold in their choice of colour. 'Black Blue' has been used on all the walls and doorframes in this magnificent hallway, creating a really dramatic dark space. As a result, all the rooms leading off the hall feel larger and lighter.

BELOW

'Card Room Green' is perfect for this charming garden room in a croft on one of the Scottish isles. By day, the room feels friendly and relaxed, in spite of the northern light. When the light fades in the evening, the paint has a surprising richness, making the room just as inviting.

FACING PAGE
Light streams through the window of this delightful east-facing breakfast room, showing off the 'Blue Gray' on the walls and the 'Off-White' on the trim to their very best advantage. Both colours look as if they have been there for ever – I can't think of a better place to start the day.

RIGHT
This is the perfect example of how a strong colour can be used in one space to make another space adjacent to it feel lighter and bigger. The diminutive staircase appears much larger than it actually is because the walls of the hall leading to it are painted in a dark 'Inchrya Blue'. 'Hardwick White' on the stairs themselves and 'Pointing' on the staircase walls serve to create an even greater sense of light and space.

STYLE

Follow your gut instinct. Choosing paint colour is as much to do with your lifestyle as with the light and the architecture of your home. It is vitally important not to just use colours that are overtly fashionable or pertinent to the date that your house was built. Choose colours that you really love and feel comfortable with. It is your home and no one else should dictate how it looks.

Work out whether you want the paint colour to be the main focus of your decoration or act purely as a backdrop. The most restful houses tend to have the same palette throughout, with one neutral family used in different ways in each room. This will provide the perfect foundation for whatever style of decor you choose.

The first impression given by your home should be welcoming, both for you and your guests. In an entrance hall, the most effective colour palettes will reflect the characters of the occupants of the house as well as its architectural features. Using a dramatic colour in the hall will create instant glamour and give you licence to make all the rooms leading off it far more neutral. The hall is the core of the house and when painted in a strong colour it makes every adjoining room look lighter and bigger. You can also afford to be a little braver in your colour choice because the hall is a room that is passed through en route to somewhere else.

Dining rooms, which are often lit by the glow of candles and chandeliers, also benefit from a bit of drama. This is best created by a stronger colour that throws the walls into shadow and leaves your table in the spotlight.

In most family houses the kitchen is the hub of the home and it is often best to make it your lightest space. Kitchens are busy places, so the same colour on both the walls and woodwork (excluding units and islands) keeps them simple and serene. This colour can also be used in the rest of the house on all other woodwork.

Bedrooms are private spaces where we go to relax, so they should be soothing and calming. To infuse a room with a sense of peace, you need to choose colours you are naturally drawn to. Reds should possibly be avoided because they are not soothing, unlike greens and blues – the colours of nature – and also neutrals, which tend to promote a sense of calm. Spare rooms, which are used less frequently, can afford to be given much more impact, by using either a strong colour or a flamboyant wallpaper. The space you create will feel like a gift to your guest.

Although many people prefer to have light bathrooms, internal spaces that rely on the walls for their colour benefit greatly from a stronger tone. Don't be scared of these smaller spaces. It is better to make them intimate and inviting, remembering that the reflective surfaces of mirrors and bathtub will bounce light around, making darker bathrooms an unexpected treat.

Be well informed and historically sensitive to your home but, more importantly, be yourself. The colours you choose, whether discreet or bold, must work for the way you live your life today. Colour can be used to define volume, shift focus and give a visual destination, but above all it should be used to make you feel that you have created a unique space that reflects your personality.

FACING PAGE
The pared-down approach to colour in this kitchen in New York has resulted in a very peaceful space. The classic colour combination of 'Drop Cloth' on the woodwork and 'Shadow White' on the walls exudes an overwhelming sense of calm and is the perfect reflection of the easy-going artist who lives here.

FOLLOWING PAGE
This 'Black Blue' hall has a really theatrical feel. You know you are somewhere special the moment you enter and it sets the scene for the other equally flamboyant rooms in the house. An added benefit of the strong colour is that it makes the rooms leading off it feel lighter and brighter.

The internal windows in this Paris home are painted in 'Pitch Black', as are the glazed doors that open out onto the courtyard garden. The walls are 'Strong White', along with the panelling glimpsed through the window, which is combined with 'Purbeck Stone' walls. Together, these colours create the perfect understated background for the owner's collection of mid-century furniture.

BELOW LEFT

The drawing room in this magnificent Georgian house in Scotland was recently painted in 'Light Gray', a bold departure from the damask-lined walls of its previous incarnation. Seen here in combination with 'Off-White' on the elaborate doorframe and panelling, the colour ensures the room retains its traditional feel but is much more suited to family life.

BELOW RIGHT

The teenage occupant of this room has chosen rich 'Brassica' as the background for a very personal collection of artwork that reflects different stages of her life. 'Pale Powder' has been used on both the trim and ceiling. By extending the ceiling colour a little way down the wall, lowering the height of the ceiling, attention is focused on the art.

FACING PAGE

The colour on the walls feels so traditional but is actually right on trend. 'Peignoir' charmingly reflects the relaxed attitude of the occupant of this Dorset cottage and creates an unpretentious interior that feels tender and nurturing. The softest of pinks, 'Peignoir' contains a big dose of grey, which makes it perfect to use alongside 'Hardwick White' on the window frame.

COLOURS

There are so many preconceptions about colour – blue is always cold, red is stimulating, yellow rooms are always welcoming and green creates restful spaces. There may be a grain of truth in all these statements but you should not get hung up on them. The mood you create in a room is most affected by the depth of colour and how that colour is used. The soft, almost imperceptible hues of 'Pink Ground', 'Tunsgate Green', 'Pavilion Blue' and 'Hound Lemon', with their crystal-clear delicacy, are sometimes almost felt rather than seen, while 'Eating Room Red', 'Green Smoke', 'Drawing Room Blue' and 'India Yellow' all ooze period grandeur.

Over the next few pages, with the help of images from houses of varying styles and eras, we explore how the five colour families of Red, Yellow, Green, Blue and Darks affect both our homes and our mood. Some schemes are clear and vivid, while others have a contemplative refinement. They are, however, all packed with beautiful colour.

FACING PAGE

My heart sings when I see this striking yet simple use of colour, which is perfect for a seaside house. 'Wimborne White' combined with 'Drawing Room Blue' has a fantastically graphic feel, creating a room that is fresh but extremely modern due to the bold move of taking the stronger colour up onto the cladding, just above the worktop. And, of course, the tin of English mustard is the perfect complementary accent.

COLOUR WHEEL

It somehow felt wrong to write this book and not include a section on the colour wheel, a tool that is so familiar to us all. However, although it is extremely useful to understand the basic structure of colour, it is not always the decorator's best friend, especially when dealing with the subtlety of the likes of the Farrow & Ball palette. Despite this, we just couldn't resist the temptation to show you Farrow & Ball's interpretation of the colour wheel in a paint kettle (see facing page).

The simple theory of the colour wheel, based on red, yellow and blue, was developed by Sir Isaac Newton in the early 18th century and was the first circular diagram of logically presented colours. The concept has been used and developed by artists and scientists ever since, creating numerous variations and even more differences of opinion.

The original wheel was made up of six sections comprising three primary colours and three secondary colours, the warmer being on one side and the cooler on the other.

Primary colours are red, blue and yellow, which cannot be created from any other colours. Secondary colours are made up of equal amounts of primary colours mixed together, creating colours like green, orange or purple: red mixed with yellow creates orange; blue mixed with yellow creates green; and red mixed with blue creates purple.

The colour wheel that we are most used to seeing today has 12 sections and includes tertiary colours, which are combinations of primary and secondary colours: yellow-green, red-orange and so on. This wheel can certainly help you to understand how colours relate to each other – those that work together and those that don't.

Colours that sit side by side are know as analogous colours, such as 'Blue Gray' and 'Mizzle', and are broadly harmonious when used together, resulting in natural-looking, tranquil spaces. You might think it would be easy to work with a scheme of harmonious colours, but careful consideration is required to avoid creating a room totally lacking in vitality when the contrasts are so subtle.

Complementary colours are any two that sit directly opposite each other on the wheel, such as 'Eating Room Red' and 'Green Smoke'. Using these creates schemes with maximum contrast, resulting in dynamic and exciting rooms with a more primal intensity. A colour scheme of complementary opposites also needs to be carefully considered to achieve a pleasing balance. When strong colours are included among them, it is often best to offset them with neutrals.

All these unfamiliar terms can be somewhat daunting and you should not get too caught up trying to remember them all. But your starting point may well be deciding whether you prefer a harmonious or a complementary scheme, and in this case the rules of the wheel can certainly be an aid in your colour selection. However, use it with caution. The infinite combinations and the relationship between colours are oversimplified in the wheel. There is so much more to creating a successful decorative scheme. Everyone's perception of colour is different and it will continue to provoke debate forever – luckily.

RED

———

Red, adored around the world from the Victorian era to the present day, is always warm and welcoming. It is also the most powerful of colours. Painting a room in red – from strong 'Radicchio', which combines a sophisticated richness with vibrant liveliness, to dusty and nostalgic 'Cinder Rose' – is not for the faint-hearted.

Strong reds are very well suited to dining rooms because they add drama and weight. Colours such as 'Eating Room Red' or 'Incarnadine', which were used originally to simulate damask, have a robust intensity and produce powerful, stimulating rooms that grab your attention. In contrast, a less vivid red will create a more restful atmosphere, as the effect of the colour strengthens over a larger area. More muted tones such as 'Book Room Red' or 'Red Earth' create warm, earthy rooms that are less challenging but still give a rich background, immediately evoking classical antiquity.

While red is sensual, pink has a gentler feel and its effect is a little more soothing. Although it is often viewed as a colour exclusively for girls, the great colourist John Fowler used pinks like 'Setting Plaster' or 'Pink Ground' extensively, creating spaces that were certainly soft but still full of impact. If, however, you want something more uplifting, then 'Nancy's Blushes' and 'Calamine' will evoke the joys of youth. Or if you feel the need for an air of nobility and splendour, then exotic 'Pelt' or 'Brinjal' will create intense and sumptuous rooms.

FACING PAGE TOP LEFT
There is a spirit of optimism in this well-lit room — you can't help but smile when greeted with the positive tones of 'Nancy's Blushes'. Pink is so often banished to the bedroom, but here you see its seductive qualities being used with great sensitivity as a background for some eclectic portraits.

FACING PAGE BOTTOM LEFT
This sitting room in a very remote farmhouse on the Scottish coast could not be warmer and more welcoming. The robust tone of 'Blazer' means that the walls have both impact and depth, along with a comforting glow that creates the perfect cocoon from the wild weather.

FACING PAGE TOP RIGHT
Exuberant 'Brinjal' has been used on both the walls and cupboards in the dressing area of this smart French chateau, creating an opulent and inviting space. Accompanied by 'Churlish Green' on the door in the foreground, this makes a classic pairing stolen directly from nature.

FACING PAGE BOTTOM RIGHT
There is something nostalgic about the dusty tones of 'Cinder Rose'. Here it is combined with 'Black Blue' on the door, creating a somewhat more modern feel but without reducing any of the romantic appeal. The combination of the paler receding colour on the walls and the advancing dark on the woodwork makes for a visually satisfying contrast.

FACING PAGE

The key to this lustrous space is that there is no contrast between the walls and the woodwork. Every element is painted the same colour — 'Book Room Red' — and even the curtain fabric has the same earthy tone as the walls. Note that the radiator is painted the same colour, so that it seemingly disappears into the wall.

THIS PAGE

'Nancy's Blushes' feels brave and bright in this vibrant bedroom, even though it has been tempered by the plain mushroom headboard and dark fur cover on the bed. All woodwork has been painted the same colour as the walls for a calming effect, while the pink has been stopped above the picture rail, making the space feel more intimate.

YELLOW

FACING PAGE

Muted 'Straw' (A) is somehow a surprising choice for the walls of this staircase, but it creates a welcoming atmosphere that has both depth and softness. The colours in the rooms leading off the hall modulate rather than contrast, providing a calm visual continuity.

Yellow has been enduringly popular since the 18th century, but it was only in the 20th century, when the influential interior designer Nancy Lancaster used the colour extensively, that it really entered the mainstream. It is still a mainstay of decoration, everywhere from rustic farmhouses to contemporary apartments, never failing to create a hopeful and optimistic atmosphere.

Yellow enhances large spaces so beautifully and creates glorious rooms that are full of energy, whether with the muted sophisticated tones of 'Sudbury Yellow' and 'Hay' or the more vibrant, clean yellows such as 'Dayroom Yellow' and 'Citron'.

Rich yellows like these can be perceived as sunshine, particularly in hallways, so they are always welcoming and have the added bonus of often making areas appear larger. Since these yellows are so stimulating, bringing rooms to life, it means they are less appropriate for the bedroom, where a soothing tone like 'Farrow's Cream' is more suitable.

Strong yellows are often best combined with a significant proportion of white to stop them being overwhelming. However, in the very modern home 'Babouche' is often used with deep, dark 'Railings' to temper its vibrant colour and create a really dramatic space. For light, refreshing rooms, it is best to combine fresh 'House White' or the slightly creamier 'New White' with crisp 'All White' on the woodwork. If you prefer a softer, more reflective room, then the combination of 'Ringwold Ground' and 'Tallow', with their slight underlying warmth, will be more restful.

PALE HOUND®   71

DAYROOM YELLOW™   233

YELLOWCAKE®   279

CITRON™   74

YELLOW GROUND™   218

BABOUCHE®   223

FACING PAGE TOP LEFT
Although yellow can sometimes appear raw in bright light, the magic of these 'India Yellow' walls is that they come into their own after dark. This exuberant Paris home is filled with colour, which makes it feel uplifting during the day and then glow at night.

FACING PAGE TOP RIGHT
This sunny bedroom painted in 'Ciara Yellow' (A) is as fresh as a spring morning. It is impossible not to feel happy and cheerful in this room with its upbeat tone and accessories that match the walls. The ceiling has been painted the same colour as the walls to prevent the slope over the bed from feeling claustrophobic.

FACING PAGE BOTTOM LEFT
'Yellowcake' was inspired by the vibrant colours used on cabinets in mid-century kitchens. Here, it has been used to stunning effect to create an upbeat washroom in a beach house. Although certainly not a colour for the faint-hearted, its boldness is most arresting.

FACING PAGE BOTTOM RIGHT
The use of 'Babouche' in this delightfully rustic bedroom is perfect to make the room feel full of energy while retaining a traditional edge. The colour was chosen particularly for the enduring warmth it gives in a north-facing room.

RIGHT
The perfectly proportioned hall of this stunning Georgian house commanded a yellow of particular sophistication. 'Print Room Yellow' (A) feels absolutely ideal, introducing comfort and warmth while flattering the historic portraits. It is complemented by 'Slipper Satin', which has a suitably aged look, on the woodwork.

GREEN

———

Green, so often associated with health and good luck, is lush and uplifting. It represents the colour of nature, from the delicate understated tones of easy-to-use 'Tunsgate Green' to the deep forest greens of the soothing 'Studio Green'.

If you have a taste for the comfortable style of the English country house, then look no further than 'Lichen' and 'Vert de Terre'. These tranquil and muted greens create rooms that are flexible and restful, as well as being the perfect backdrop to shabby chic furniture and well-loved fabrics. They are best used with a traditional white like 'Lime White' or 'Off-White' to soften the contrast between walls and woodwork.

For a more upbeat room, you need to opt for a more vital green like the sparkling 'Cooking Apple Green' or 'Green Ground'. These colours often feature in kitchens because their refreshing, outdoorsy feel gives rooms breathing space and creates a happy family atmosphere. For a more sophisticated look, 'Ball Green', an old distemper colour, has a magical quality, appearing almost silver in candlelight, which make it perfect for dining rooms, along with the darker but equally smoky 'Card Room Green'.

In one of the earliest recorded references to painted decoration, Henry III ordered that the panelling in his principal residence at Windsor be painted green. Whether this was to promote a feeling of health and vigour or to reflect the balanced feeling of nature is unknown, but to this day green rooms retain an essence of life unmatched by any other colour.

FACING PAGE
This rural kitchen is the natural home for 'Breakfast Room Green', where it is full of life by day as well as by candlelight. It is also the perfect complement to the cream-coloured vintage range. This mid-tone green always creates the most comfortable of environments and it can be used in both contemporary and traditional homes to the same effect.

BELOW LEFT
Although muted in colour, 'Lichen' feels sophisticated and unapologetically clubby in this Paris sitting room. It is the perfect example of how wall colour can contribute to the creation of a really alluring retreat. Here, it works particularly well in combination with the gilded mirror and marble fireplace, which both provide warmth and balance.

BELOW RIGHT
The vintage dresser in this rural kitchen has been lovingly restored, with its exterior painted in sober 'Calke Green'. Refreshing 'Cooking Apple Green' has been used on the inside, to create depth and provide the perfect background for a display of chinaware.

BLUE

When it comes to decorating, blue tends to divide opinion more than any other colour. For some it immediately conjures up cold, unfriendly spaces, while for others it evokes calm and serenity.

The price of blue pigment once exceeded that of gold, but now the colour is more widely used in decoration than any other. It reflects the soothing tones of both the sea and the sky, creating rooms with a timeless appeal. The aqua qualities of 'Pale Powder' and 'Dix Blue', with their underlying green, produce pretty spaces that could never be seen as cold, making them perfect colours for bedrooms and bathrooms. The more airy 'Borrowed Light' and 'Parma Gray' certainly feel cooler. However, when combined with clean white, they create the freshest of rooms, reminiscent of the colours of Wedgwood china – formal without being stuffy.

The most relaxed and easy-to-use blues are those that lean towards grey. From deepest 'Pigeon' to softest 'Cromarty', these shades work together seamlessly in any combination.

If you are unafraid of strong, clean colours, then 'St Giles Blue', with its vibrant zing, is life-enhancing in bright light, but in more diffused light it becomes softer and more comforting, as do 'Cook's Blue' and 'Blue Ground'. Meanwhile, the darker, more sophisticated blues like 'Hague Blue' and 'Stiffkey Blue', which create a really dramatic, glamorous feel, have increased in popularity as an alternative to charcoal grey.

Cleopatra is said to have used pure ground lapis lazuli as eyeshadow. Indeed, blue is often thought of as regal, but it should also be viewed as calm and spiritual when used in the home.

FACING PAGE
'Stiffkey Blue' manages to feel both dramatic and optimistic in this simply decorated space. The drama comes from its unrivalled depth of colour, inspired by the mud and sand of a north Norfolk beach, while its freshness is derived from 'All White' being used on the trim and echoed in the bright white lampshade.

BELOW LEFT

'Lulworth Blue', a clean mid-tone Regency blue, is an excellent choice for this fresh-feeling seaside bedroom. Not only does the colour emulate the sea and the sky, but it also has an unsurpassed vigour that makes for a delightfully upbeat room, especially when contrasted with bright white bedding.

BELOW MIDDLE

The use of powerfully intense 'Inchyra Blue' on the walls with an 'Off-Black' trim gives an old-fashioned solidity and a sense of drama. 'Cook's Blue' on the door tempers this dark-on-dark scheme, adding a vibrant extra element.

BELOW RIGHT

'Green Blue' feels modest and retiring in this traditional bedroom. Although ostensibly blue, its green undertones mean that it never feels cold. Here, it is the perfect counterpoint to the red of the bedcover, which is the main focal point of this perfectly balanced room.

FACING PAGE

It is the uncomplicated nature of this sitting room, painted in clean blue 'Parma Gray', that makes it so attractive. Bright 'All White' used on the bookcase and lamp base means that you perceive more colour on the walls — a perfect example of how sometimes 'less is more'.

DARKS

MAHOGANY™ 36

TANNER'S BROWN® 255

RAILINGS™ 31

BLACK BLUE™ 95

OFF-BLACK™ 57

PITCH BLACK™ 256

Over the past decade it seems that many designers have crossed over to the dark side for their paint colours. People are less concerned about space and more concerned with mood, with the result that deep, saturated colours like 'Mahogany' and 'Black Blue' abound.

Although such shades are possibly not the first you would gravitate to, they can be an inspired solution in dark spaces, blurring boundaries so you can't read the perimeters of the room. However, even in larger, more open spaces, dark tones can flatter a room's proportions; a very large-scale room may command a strong colour such as 'Plummett' or 'Tanner's Brown'. Rooms painted in these seemingly simple colours evoke a complex response. They are, of course, undeniably moody, but they have an unexpected hint of modernity about them, especially when only one colour is used on all the elements in the room.

Deep, rich shades like 'Pelt' and 'London Clay' serve as the perfect background for home furnishings, and their warm undertone gives them a softness, making them soothing and romantic in bedrooms. Commanding 'Mole's Breath' and 'Off-Black' are more flattering to adjacent colours than an intense jet black, so are perfect in rooms that double up as living spaces and media rooms.

From the muted grey tone of 'Down Pipe' to the complex black-blue of 'Railings', darks are respectful of traditional proportions but can also create modern and dynamic spaces in the contemporary home.

FACING PAGE
Most of the rooms in this super-stylish Dutch house are either painted white or in saturated darks, depending on the orientation of the space. 'Black Blue', used here on both the walls and the trim, is a wise choice, as any thin white lines around the room, whether on the skirting/baseboard or the dado rail, would ruin the streamlined effect.

The hall in my house has been painted in 'Down Pipe' for 15 years, which is a record, considering that every other room has been painted at least 15 times. The colour's enduring appeal comes from the sense of drama it provides when one enters the space, as well as the fact that it makes all the rooms off the hall feel huge and full of light. The floor and bench are painted in 'Strong White'. I couldn't resist adding some extra colour in the form of a little yarn bombing on my bench.

LEFT
This industrial steel dresser deserves a powerful backdrop, and rich 'Railings', being neither black nor blue, is the perfect complement. When using any dark colour on the wall, it is popular to paint the woodwork the same hue, as here — all the better for creating a really striking space.

ABOVE
This combination of 'Mole's Breath' on the walls and 'Off-Black' on the floor and window frames is deliciously handsome. Although grey, 'Mole's Breath' contains fewer blue undertones than many other darks, so is a little warmer in feel — the perfect colour for the modern dark room.

THIS PAGE
Although this Brooklyn hall has an air of simplicity about it, the colours on the walls and trim work deceptively well together. Cool, grey 'Dimpse' is used on the panelling and walls, while the doors are painted in its lighter counterpart, 'Blackened'. These Architectural Neutrals sit perfectly with the grey oak floor, to create a modern, clean-feeling space.

NEUTRALS

There is no doubt that neutrals have been the most popular tones for home use during the first decades of the 21st century – and perhaps for good reason. Many people feel most comfortable when surrounded by carefully balanced colours that create an understated environment and make few demands on the eye. Neutrals offer infinite possibilities for making spaces airy and relaxing, refined and timeless, or elegantly sophisticated. However, neutrals alone are not a fail-safe combination and it is all too easy to fall into the trap of using bland, depressing colours that are nothing like the subtle, complex palettes featured here.

Light plays a huge part in how neutrals appear, which is why Farrow & Ball has created six neutral groups – Traditional, Yellow-based, Red-based, Contemporary, Easy and Architectural – for every light condition. Although each group creates a very different look, they can be relied upon to work perfectly together, in seemingly endless permutations.

Selecting a neutral group is easy – simply consider the light in the room and decide which group you are most drawn to. When you have established your preferred neutral tones, you can then build a decorating scheme, possibly with the addition of bolder colours and wallpapers to flow throughout your home.

Older or classic buildings tend to demand softer effects from neutrals and are most suited to the Traditional, Yellow-based and Red-based Neutrals. More contemporary settings benefit from the subtle, tone-on-tone harmonious greys of the Contemporary, Easy and Architectural Neutrals.

TRADITIONAL NEUTRALS

This inimitable group of neutral shades has its roots firmly in the past – they were the first 'whites' created by Farrow & Ball and still result in a very special atmosphere. The most traditional in feel of our neutral groups, they create calm, restrained spaces that still have an unmatched richness and depth. Deemed to be extremely sophisticated, they have been used everywhere from the decorative plaster ceilings of 18th-century historic houses to vast Parisian apartments. However, these Traditional Neutrals are just as suited to 'downstairs' situations and are the perfect tones for boot rooms and garden rooms.

Wherever they are used, their complex underlying grey-green tones have a softness that produces decorative schemes that feel as if they have been there forever. If used in spaces starved of light or that face north (in the northern hemisphere), the underlying green may be more prominent, making them feel all the more historic.

One of the most effective ways to use Traditional Neutrals is to have them all in one room, layered one upon another: the mid-colour 'Off-White' on the walls, the darker 'Old White' on the woodwork, 'Lime White' on any moulding or coving and 'Slipper Satin' on the ceiling. This will result in an area that feels seamlessly sophisticated and relaxed in equal measure.

'Lime White'

'Off-White'

'Slipper Satin'

'Old White'

'Lime White'

'Off-White'

'Slipper Satin'

'Old White'

'Slipper Satin'

'Old White'

YELLOW-BASED NEUTRALS

In recent years, many people have turned their back on any colour construed to be 'yellow'. However, the Yellow-based Neutrals should never be thought of as yellow – they are more complex in colour and have a delicacy and a lightness of touch that is unmatchable. Their traditional feel stems from the addition of a minute amount of black, which takes them from the ordinary to the special.

The Yellow-based Neutrals are the prettiest and simplest of the neutral groups. Their roots are in the country and they work perfectly in any rustic situation. They can grace the most delicate of rooms because they are so easy to live with. Like the Traditional Neutrals, they can appear a little green in northern light, where it may be preferable to use the warmer 'Tallow', 'Ringwold Ground' or 'Savage Ground', which have a natural reflective quality.

The most flattering and subtle use of neutrals takes into account the surrounding landscape, and the Yellow-based Neutrals are perfect for sunny garden rooms, where they will enhance the connection between exterior and interior. Earthy 'String' is a natural colour for conservatory woodwork, while the walls might be painted in 'Matchstick', to create a quiet stillness, and the furniture in a mix of fresh 'New White' and 'White Tie'.

'New White'

'White Tie'

'String'

'Matchstick'

'White Tie'

'New White'

'String'

'Matchstick'

RED-BASED NEUTRALS

Neutrals are at their best when used with others of a similar tone, and the unassuming colours of the Red-based Neutrals sit perfectly together to create ageless and understated colour schemes. Their red base produces the warmest schemes of all the neutrals.

These tones were used originally in the 17th century to mimic the colour of whatever the paint was covering, be it plaster, stone or wood, but they were revived in response to the overwhelming desire for 'taupe' in recent decades.

These neutrals are particularly useful in contemporary classic homes – they make the perfect pairings with many popular decorating materials such as linen, leather and limestone. It is so often the layering of these colours, in paint or in furnishings, that keeps the palette alive. The colours also work beautifully in traditional situations and are particularly suited to underlit spaces, creating serene interiors with unmatchable warmth.

The welcoming, friendly colours of the Red-based Neutrals are perfect for exteriors, too. The strongest, 'Oxford Stone', reminiscent of the colour of stone used in traditional Cotswolds houses, is a natural choice for masonry, while the slightly lighter 'Joa's White' sits perfectly alongside on quoins and fascia boards. 'Dimity' could then be used on window frames, with delicate 'Pointing' on glazing bars, to create the most seamless and undemanding of schemes.

'Pointing'

'Dimity'

'Joa's White'

'Oxford Stone'

'Oxford Stone'

CONTEMPORARY NEUTRALS

The grey interior became achingly fashionable at the beginning of the 21st century. Although the Farrow & Ball Traditional Neutrals were already seen by many as grey, these Contemporary Neutrals have a much cleaner, more urban feel – with a contemporary twist. The magic of the group lies in the fact that all the colours have an underlying lilac tone, which brings an edge to decorative schemes while imparting a certain warmth. This undertone also prevents them from ever appearing sombre or severe, so they are perfect in the modern family home, where they will never have the gritty, industrial feel of colder, bluer greys. They are enriching shades that flatter each other, and have a refined sophistication while remaining understated.

The Contemporary Neutral group is often used throughout an entire house, so you can drift from room to room hardly noticing that there has been a change in shade. The strongest tone, 'Elephant's Breath', could feature in the hall, to create a sense of drama upon entering the house, while 'Skimming Stone' will make living areas feel as light as possible. 'Strong White' is regularly used in kitchens, where it feels a natural choice alongside steel fittings, and will make the room the most airy in the house. 'All White' could then be used on all ceilings, to provide continuity.

EASY NEUTRALS

These neutrals have a gossamer appearance, which is ideal for anyone who prefers understated decoration. For many, this harmonious group creates a look that is ultimately easy to live with and will sit happily in almost any home. It does not challenge us very much but gives a huge amount of versatility, resulting in the perfect environment for relaxation.

The Easy Neutrals are neither too grey to be edgy and uncomfortable, nor too creamy to feel out of date. They have no bias to either warmer or cooler tones and can be used in virtually any combination. They will slightly soften contemporary architectural settings and also provide strong foundations for all the other Farrow & Ball colours. Many people interpret them as having their roots in the much admired Gustavian palette. They are natural and quiet, with a quality that is hard to pin down but always results in a comforting space.

'Purbeck Stone' used on the walls, with 'Cornforth White' woodwork and 'Ammonite' on the ceiling will create the subtlest of looks, almost as if you have used only one colour and the differences in tone are shadows. The minimal aesthetic of this combination will promote simple, calm, easy modern living, which is the perfect antidote to the chaos of modern life.

'Ammonite'

'Wevet'

'Cornforth White'

'Purbeck Stone'

'Wevet'

'Cornforth White'

'Ammonite'

'Purbeck Stone'

'Purbeck Stone'

ARCHITECTURAL NEUTRALS

This is the ideal group for those wanting a strong architectural or modern industrial feel. Purposely cool, with a bluer undertone than the other neutral families, the Architectural Neutrals give a more hard-edged look that is conducive to minimal living.

The Architectural Neutrals are a great alternative to the pure white so favoured by architects, which can be almost blindingly stark. With the addition of almost imperceptible quantities of other pigments, these greys take on a completely new personality, creating a sense of spaciousness while avoiding an unforgiving clinical look. They are definitely the right colours for those who believe in the 'less is more' school of decorating. However, they should not be considered solely for modern glass boxes; they can be fabulously elegant when combined with a simple, clean white in more traditional houses.

By nature of their strong architectural feel, the Architectural Neutrals are most often used with the lightest tone, 'Blackened', on both the walls and ceilings throughout the entire house, to create a light and seamless space. The strongest tone, 'Manor House Gray', would then feature on the floors to ground the scheme, with 'Dimpse' and 'Pavilion Gray' used in small rooms, as accents or on furniture.

SAMPLING

There is something intrinsically pleasing about the perfectly proportioned Farrow & Ball sample pot, so much so that it has become an iconic image for contemporary decorating. I have seen them everywhere, from pristine architects' offices, where they were precision-stacked, to garage sales, where big baskets of them were on offer to the chance decorator. Many get washed out to be used as pencil pots, and one was even used to present an engagement ring to an unsuspecting Farrow & Ball fan.

The real jewels, however, are the 132 inimitable Farrow & Ball colours for which these little pots were originally made. Although our colour cards are created with real paint (no printing for Farrow & Ball), there is no substitute for testing proposed colours in the room to be decorated. The reasons for recommending this so strongly are as follows:

First, our paint is full of wonderful pigment that is very susceptible to changes in the light. The fact that the colour on the walls alters when a cloud passes over the sun and looks different throughout the day or even across the seasons is what makes the paint feel alive. It is this quality that gives an interior a unique sense of depth and atmosphere.

Second, it is preferable to look at the colour in the correct light. If you are decorating a space used exclusively at night, such as a dining room, you may want to view the colour by candlelight.

Third, it is often useful to see the colour in relation to the decorative scheme of an adjoining space – these subtle tones are best perceived in context rather than in isolation. They will always be affected by the colours used next to them, whether in the house or the sampling process. For example, a strong red tested against a white background may appear somewhat duller than if it is tested against black, where it will look more brilliant.

The golden rule about sampling is not to paint directly onto the wall about to be decorated, no matter how tempting that might be. This is because the new colour will be directly affected by the existing colour – the very one you are trying to get rid of. You should compare new colours with the decorative elements that are staying, not with the old paint colour that is about to disappear. Rejected colour samples are not only very distracting but are also a bore to paint over if they are on the wall – graffiti can be eye-catching but not in the home!

If you want to sample several colours, it is even more important to look at them in isolation. If you paint them in a patchwork on the wall, each one will influence the other, which makes it incredibly difficult to get a real sense of what the colour will look like when it is on its own.

If you are sampling a colour destined for the wall alongside a colour for the woodwork, remember to look at them proportionally – there will be a much greater amount of the colour chosen for the walls colour than for the trim, and this will affect the way you perceive both tones.

Paint the contents of a sample pot onto two pieces of paper or card – the larger, the better – and place them in two different areas of the room to be decorated. Remember that you will only see the true colour if you apply two coats of paint on your samples. Then look at how the colour changes at different times of the day – check them in the evening light as well as during the day to ensure you obtain your desired look.

How a colour behaves in relation to other colours and in different light conditions is extremely complex and nothing beats seeing them all in situ. And the added bonus is that you will have all those iconic little pots to treasure.

THIS PAGE
Here, the Easy Neutrals are being sampled in a bright, undecorated space. The intention is to use all three colours — 'Purbeck Stone' 'Cornforth White' and accent colour, 'Mole's Breath' — in combination on the walls, woodwork and fire surround.

Four wallpapers — clockwise from top left, 'Peony' (BP 2302), 'Versailles' (BP 2602), 'Silvergate' (BP 803) and 'St Antoine' (BP 909) — are also being considered for the chimneybreast. They each have their individual charms.

PART TWO

—

THE MANUAL

FACING PAGE
There is something effortlessly pleasing about the combination of 'Mole's Breath', on the panelling, and 'Ammonite', on the walls, in this dining room. Using the darker colour on the panelling means that the lighter walls open out, making the room feel bigger and more airy.

95

WHICH WHITE?

———

Even after making the painstaking decision as to which colour to use on the walls, there are many of us who are equally blinded by the range of whites for ceilings and trim. The following is a very simple list of the most appropriate white to use with each Farrow & Ball colour – there are many whites that work with most colours, depending on whether you want a subtle, muted feel or a fresh, graphic scheme. But whatever your desired look, the colours outlined below are designed to make life easier, and you can use them in total confidence, knowing that they will complement your chosen colour.

A

All White / Strong White
Ammonite / Wevet
Archive / Dimity
Arsenic / All White

B

Babouche / House White
Ball Green / James White
Black Blue / Ammonite
Blackened / All White
Blazer / Joa's White
Blue Gray / Shaded White
Blue Ground / Pointing
Bone / Lime White
Book Room Red / Dimity
Borrowed Light / All White
Brassica / Great White
Breakfast Room Green / James White
Brinjal / Skimming Stone

C

Cabbage White / All White
Calamine / Great White
Calke Green / Slipper Satin

Calluna / Wimborne White
Card Room Green / Lime White
Charleston Gray / Skimming Stone
Charlotte's Locks / All White
Churlish Green / James White
Cinder Rose / Great White
Citron / House White
Clunch / Wimborne White
Cooking Apple Green / James White
Cook's Blue / All White
Cord / New White
Cornforth White / Wevet
Cromarty / Shadow White

D

Dayroom Yellow / Wimborne White
Dead Salmon / Dimity
Dimity / Pointing
Dimpse / All White
Dix Blue / Clunch
Dorset Cream / New White
Dove Tale / Strong White
Down Pipe / Dimpse
Drawing Room Blue / Blackened
Drop Cloth / Shadow White

E

Eating Room Red / Joa's White
Elephant's Breath / Strong White

F

Farrow's Cream / White Tie
French Gray / Lime White

G

Great White / All White
Green Blue / Pointing
Green Ground / James White
Green Smoke / Off-White

H

Hague Blue / Old White
Hardwick White / Clunch
Hay / James White
House White / All White

I

Incarnadine / Wimborne White
Inchyra Blue / Shaded White
India Yellow / Matchstick

J

James White / All White
Joa's White / Dimity

L

Lamp Room Gray / Strong White
Lichen / Lime White
Light Blue / Strong White
Light Gray / Clunch
Lime White / Slipper Satin
London Clay / Skimming Stone
London Stone / Joa's White
Lulworth Blue / All White

M

Mahogany / Joa's White
Manor House Gray / Blackened
Matchstick / White Tie
Middleton Pink / All White
Mizzle / Wimborne White
Mole's Breath / Ammonite
Mouse's Back / Off-White

N

Nancy's Blushes / Great White
New White / White Tie

O

Off-Black / Dimpse
Off-White / Slipper Satin
Old White / Slipper Satin
Oval Room Blue / Shadow White
Oxford Stone / Dimity

P

Pale Hound / Wimborne White
Pale Powder / Pointing
Parma Gray / Wimborne White
Pavilion Blue / All White
Pavilion Gray / Blackened
Peignoir / Wimborne White
Pelt / Great White
Picture Gallery Red / Joa's White
Pigeon / Shaded White
Pink Ground / Tallow
Pitch Black / Shadow White
Pitch Blue / Blackened
Plummett / Ammonite
Pointing / Wimborne White
Purbeck Stone / Wevet

R

Radicchio / Joa's White
Railings / Ammonite
Rectory Red / Dimity
Red Earth / Dimity
Ringwold Ground / Tallow

S

Salon Drab / Dimity
Savage Ground / New White
Setting Plaster / Tallow
Shaded White / Shadow White
Shadow White / Wimborne White
Skimming Stone / Strong White
Skylight / All White
Slipper Satin / Pointing

Smoked Trout / Dimity
St Giles Blue / All White
Stiffkey Blue / Shadow White
Stone Blue / Strong White
Stony Ground / Slipper Satin
String / White Tie
Strong White / All White
Studio Green / Lime White
Sudbury Yellow / New White

T

Tallow / Pointing
Tanner's Brown / Joa's White
Teresa's Green / Slipper Satin
Tunsgate Green / All White

V

Vardo / Shaded White
Vert de Terre / Slipper Satin

W

Wevet / All White
White Tie / Wimborne White
Wimborne White / All White
Worsted / Shadow White

Y

Yeabridge Green / James White
Yellowcake / All White
Yellow Ground / White Tie

COVERAGE

PAINT

Not ordering enough paint for your decorating project can be very frustrating, and ordering too much will mean you're left with items you don't need. You can minimize the chances of this happening by using the convenient paint calculator below, but please take into account the nature of the surface that you are painting – remember, it is only designed to help you with the amount you need for walls. Porous surfaces are likely to require extra coats, while vast colour transformations (such as white to black, or black to white) are also likely to require a third coat. You can minimize the chances of this by using the correct Primer and Undercoat.

WALLPAPER

Ordering too much wallpaper is equally frustrating, although when calculating the number of rolls to buy, we will always recommend including an extra one in case of accidents when hanging, or for repairs, as the colour may change between batches if you need to order more in the future. Leftover wallpaper can always be used inside cupboards or to line drawers as an unexpected treat.

Each roll is 10m (32 ft) long and 53cm (21 in) wide. The best way to work out how many rolls of wallpaper you need is to ask your paper hanger. Alternatively, Farrow & Ball can help you estimate your requirement, although our advice is for guidance only.

Paint type	Approximate coverage*
Estate Emulsion	70m² per 5 litres
Modern Emulsion	60m² per 5 litres
Estate Eggshell	60m² per 5 litres
Floor Paint	60m² per 5 litres
Full Gloss	30m² per 2.5 litres
Dead Flat	60m² per 5 litres
Exterior Masonry	40m² per 5 litres
Exterior Eggshell	32m² per 2.5 litres
Casein Distemper	65m² per 5 litres
Soft Distemper	65m² per 5 litres
Limewash	Varies on condition

*Coverage outlined above is reflective of the largest tin size available. For readers in the US requiring tin sizes in imperial units, please refer to www.farrow-ball.com

FACING PAGE
The use of my favourite wallpaper, 'Tessella' (BP 3604), in this dining area is a brave choice. It complements the floor tiles in both rooms, while the 'Dayroom Yellow' painted on the table gives the whole space a lighter touch.

WAYS OF
DECORATING

Every room should be seen as a fantastic opportunity to use colour. Whether your choice of scheme has been spontaneous and instinctive, or heartfelt and studied, it is only the beginning of your journey towards making the most of your particular space.

When faced with a room made up of seemingly complicated architectural elements, it can be a little overwhelming choosing where each colour should go. Your first decision is whether the woodwork should be highlighted or not. This will probably be influenced by the style of your room. Most people default to the classic preference of using a clean white trim in traditional rooms, where there has always been a presumption that woodwork should be painted lighter than the walls. In contemporary rooms, on the other hand, where the trim is usually less decorative, it is often thought best to paint everything in one colour to create a backdrop that is more conducive to minimal living.

Although it may feel as if the possibilities are endless, it is comforting to remember that there are three basic ways of decorating: light on dark; dark on light; and one colour throughout.

LIGHT ON DARK

The first method of decorating, and the most traditional, is to use a colour on the walls and a white on the woodwork. Using white gloss became almost standard for many years, before its perceived austerity made it fall out of favour. Things have come full circle, though, and it is extremely popular once more, beloved for its freshness, crisp contrast and simplicity. Used throughout a house, it also unifies and connects all the rooms.

A bright white, however, can totally destroy a room when there are muted, subtle colours on the walls, and this is where the Farrow & Ball whites are second to none. For every colour, there is a sympathetic white, be it 'James White' to go with greens, or warm 'Dimity' to go with reds. There is a lot to be gained by using a white that is more sympathetic to the wall colour, as this creates a softer, more airy atmosphere. If the contrast between your walls and woodwork is strong, your eye will be drawn to that line of contrast and you will become very aware of each architectural element. When you are conscious of where the skirting/baseboard, doors and windows are, it makes the room feel smaller by defining the space. If these features are all softened by a white that sits tonally with the colour of the wall, you will notice them less and the room will feel bigger and calmer. These tone-on-tone schemes create quieter, more seamless rooms.

RIGHT
This charming, airy bathroom has been painted in the most traditional and uncomplicated way. A wash of colour is achieved by using 'Pale Powder' on the walls, complemented by lighter 'Pointing' on all the woodwork.

FACING PAGE
'Dead Salmon', a colour discovered at Kedleston Hall, Derbyshire, feels strangely modern in this pared-down room. It is used with 'Dimity' on the woodwork, a sympathetic white from the Red-based Neutrals. The two sit seamlessly together, a perfect example of how a Farrow & Ball white can soften the edges between walls and trim.

ABOVE LEFT

Who could resist this light-filled bathroom in New York State? The combination of 'Middleton Pink' on the walls and 'All White' on the woodwork reminds us of the uncomplicated days of childhood, and feels fresh and pretty to boot.

LEFT

This quiet corner in a Dutch house is unified by the use of 'Wevet' on the expansive woodwork. This delicate white, with its hint of grey, is the perfect colour alongside 'Lamp Room Gray' on the walls. The fact that the two have the same base tone means they sit seamlessly together.

ABOVE

The combination of 'Teresa's Green' on the walls and 'Pointing' on the woodwork is totally classic and utterly fitting for the magnificent landing of this historic house. Very often simple schemes such as these are the most effective.

FACING PAGE

This room exudes an amazing sense of calm. The walls are 'Skimming Stone', which is the perfect grey for bedrooms because it never feels too cold. Here, it is combined with the lighter 'Wimborne White' on both the woodwork and the floor to retain a feeling of crispness and simplicity.

DARK ON LIGHT

The second method of decorating is to make your trim darker than the walls. Most people want to create as much light and space in a room as they can, and using a lighter colour on the walls, which is the biggest space, with a darker tone on the woodwork, is the easiest way to achieve this. The dark trim instantly makes the walls feel lighter and adds a decorative element to your scheme. While this may feel like an intimidating prospect, remember how easily we accept rooms in which the woodwork is unpainted, maybe a rich mahogany or a plain pine. That thought just has to be transferred into paint colour.

The use of a very slightly darker colour on the woodwork than on the walls is a method often seen in Regency houses, providing simple decoration while maintaining a degree of calm. Again, the Farrow & Ball palette, with its multitude of colours that sit together so seamlessly, is perfect for this. Using a strong colour on woodwork with pale walls, a combination so popular with the Victorians, has had a great resurgence in popularity. It creates drama and is ideal if you wish to make a bold statement on a smaller scale. However, it can create a barrier between rooms, as it has the effect of drawing a frame around each space. These dark architectural elements draw the eye to them, changing both the room's focal point and its sense of scale, so you should be careful not to let them become overwhelming.

RIGHT
The use of 'Hague Blue' on the woodwork of this children's bathroom in a townhouse in Bath introduces a whole new, and very modern, element. With 'Pink Ground' on the walls, 'Setting Plaster' on the vanity unit and 'Strong White' on the floor, this makes for a charming and unusual scheme.

FACING PAGE
Using a lighter colour on the walls than on the woodwork makes a room feel bigger and more airy. Here, choosing 'Ammonite' for the walls and the slightly darker 'Purbeck Stone' on the trim achieves this perfectly. The dark door painted in 'Down Pipe' enhances the overall effect.

ABOVE LEFT
In the garden room of this French chateau, 'Pale Hound' on the walls sits perfectly with the colour of the tiled floor. The stronger, but equally soft, 'Lamp Room Gray' on the double doors gives them the importance they deserve, as well as introducing you to the bolder colours that have been used in the adjoining room.

ABOVE RIGHT
The effortless combination of 'Shadow White' on the walls and its stronger counterpart 'Drop Cloth' on the woodwork, has been used to great effect in the hall of this Dorset cottage, making it feel both relaxed and carefully considered. Although the darker woodwork is not immediately noticeable, this space would be far duller without it.

ABOVE LEFT
Delicate 'Borrowed Light'
on the walls has been
grounded by 'Stiffkey Blue'
on the skirting/baseboard,
which creates the perfect
counterbalance to the
'Wimborne White' used above
the picture rail. This scheme
is a great favourite for
children's bedrooms but it
is equally effective in this
calm dining room.

ABOVE RIGHT
This is one of my favourite
uses of space. There is
enough room in this very
large kitchen to transform
a corner of it into a study
area. The cosy look has
been achieved by painting
the impressive window
frame, glazing bars and
shutters in 'Stone Blue',
which stand out against the
walls of 'New White'.

ONE COLOUR

The third method of decorating is to use one colour on both the walls and woodwork. There is great historic precedent for this form of decorating. Much used by the Georgians, it has become a firm favourite with many contemporary decorators because rooms painted in this way are both tranquil and extremely chic.

Panelling, traditionally picked out in three colours, becomes elegant and simple when painted in only one. When a single colour is used, a room suddenly feels bigger, because having no contrast means that you are less aware of the confines of the space. This creates a feeling of openness and simplicity, and makes the perfect backdrop for displaying art.

Many people are scared of using dark colours on woodwork, particularly windows, but it is amazing how natural it feels, even if the colour is strong. Ugly, small or plain trim disappears into the wall colour and you really only notice the shadow that it casts. Another bonus of using one colour is that it connects the interior with the exterior, blending the garden and room together. If your window woodwork is the same colour as the walls, the eye does not stop to register a second colour and glides straight out to the view.

The wall colour is certainly the most important choice and will always dominate the room, but you also need to decide whether to hide or highlight the trim. Remember, there are three ways, as described in this chapter, to tackle this age-old problem.

RIGHT
Effortless chic is achieved in this room within a classic Dutch house by using dramatic 'Railings' on all the surfaces, except the ceiling. This method of decorating creates strong, calm spaces. It can also be used to cover up a multitude of sins, such as mismatched trim, and it even hides the door hinges.

FACING PAGE
This beautiful room has been painted in 'Pavilion Gray' to maximize the light. This would be far less effective if the doors were not the same colour as the wall, as they virtually disappear into it with no distraction. Pretty 'Calamine' has been used to emphasize the unusual recess and pottery collection.

ABOVE LEFT

Here, a room painted entirely
in 'Tanner's Brown' leads
on to another painted in the
slightly more vibrant 'Oval
Room Blue'. Many people worry
about doors being painted
different colours on each
side. However, when the
execution is this good,
it feels entirely natural.

ABOVE RIGHT

Like many bedrooms, this
spectacular example in a
Toronto house has doors
that lead to other rooms.
To retain the size and impact
of the room, the confident
owners painted not only
the walls, but also the
panelling, architraves and,
most importantly, the doors

in the same strong, fairly
acid 'Citron'. The end
result is a fantastically
chic space.

ABOVE LEFT

The obviously confined space of a houseboat means that it is essential to paint the same colour on the wall cladding and the window, in order to make the room feel as big as possible. 'Cornforth White' has been used everywhere, except on the ceiling, where the much lighter 'All White' bounces any available light around the room. The darker 'Purbeck Stone' on the floor grounds the space.

ABOVE RIGHT

Every surface in this room, from the walls and doors to the radiator and window, has been painted in 'Blackened'. The coolest of all our whites, it creates a look that is both seamless and calm, and makes the perfect backdrop for bursts of colour in the furniture and art.

113

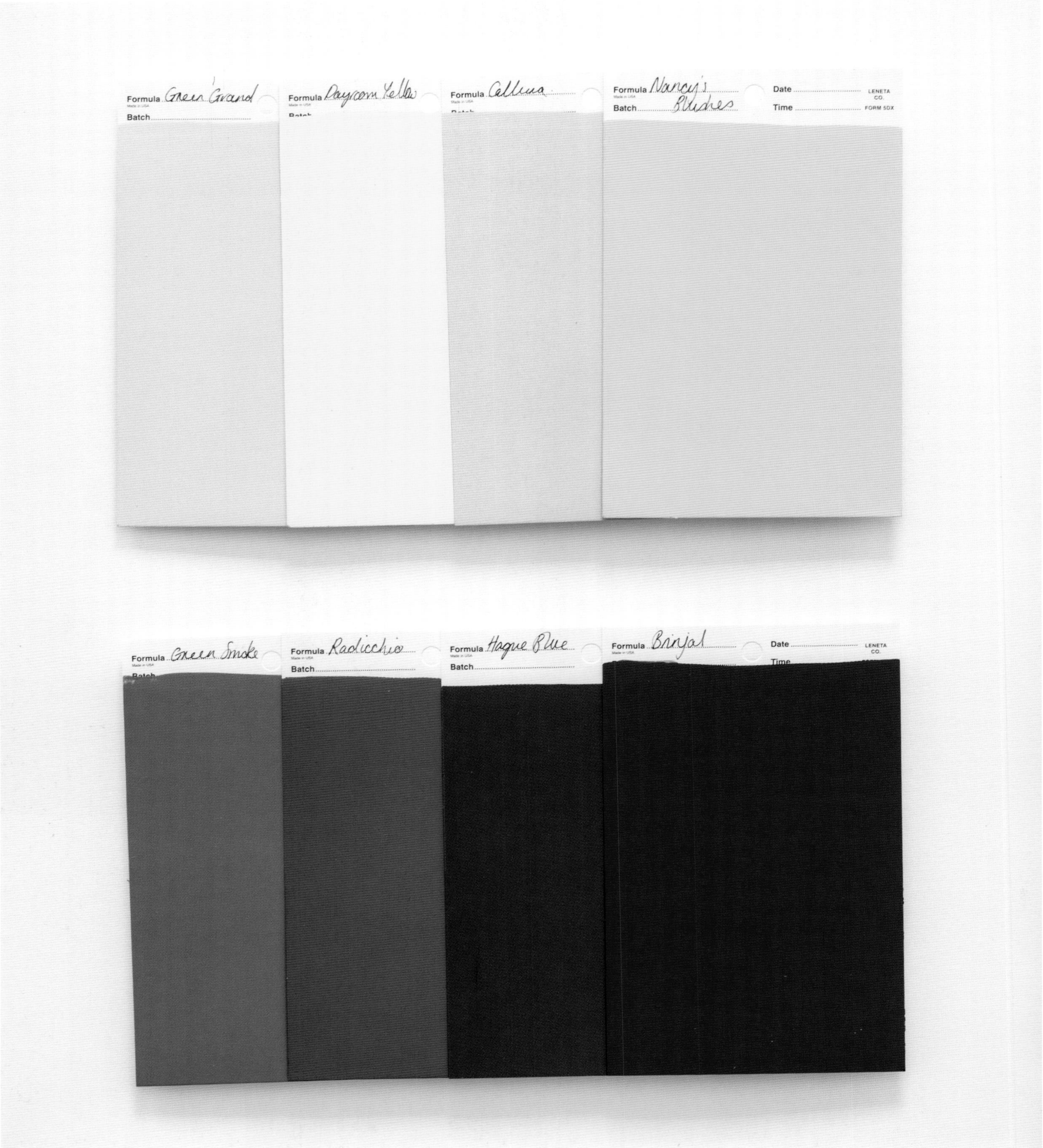

Formula *Green Grand*
Made in USA
Batch

Formula *Daygrom Yellow*
Made in USA
Batch

Formula *Calluna*
Batch

Formula *Nancy's Blushes*
Made in USA
Batch

Date
Time

LENETA
CO.

FORM 5DX

Formula *Green Smoke*
Made in USA
Batch

Formula *Radicchio*
Made in USA
Batch

Formula *Hague Blue*
Made in USA
Batch

Formula *Brinjal*
Made in USA

Date
Time

LENETA
CO.

FLOW

In this day and age, most people want to create a flow through their home. They see it as paramount in producing an unchallenging environment, where you can drift from room to room without being jolted by the use of colour. As outlined below, this can be achieved in a number of ways, whether you want a pared-down, simple feel or a fantastic riot of colour.

One colour or one group of neutrals
One ceiling colour
One woodwork colour
Tone-on-tone colour
Several colours
A unifying hall colour

FACING PAGE
The lighter shades of 'Green Ground', 'Dayroom Yellow', 'Calluna' and 'Nancy's Blushes' sit seamlessly together, as do the darker, but equally weighted 'Green Smoke', 'Radicchio', 'Hague Blue' and 'Brinjal'.

THIS PAGE AND FACING PAGE
The fact that only two
colours, 'Lamp Room Gray'
and 'Wimborne White', are
used in these three rooms
means that their choice was
critical. The colours have
to succeed in three different
light conditions, as well as
work with varying styles of
architecture. In the sitting
area (left), they need to be
strong enough to create an
intimate atmosphere; in the
simpler dining area (below
left), light and modern
enough to enhance the space;
and in the kitchen, the right
level of colour to complement
the more embellished walls.

ONE COLOUR OR ONE GROUP OF NEUTRALS

Creating a flow through the home can, of course, be easily achieved with just one colour. This approach has been much encouraged by contemporary architects, who prefer the eye to be caught by the line of the architecture rather than any form of colour.

White, often considered the colour of perfection, would inevitably be the first shade to turn to – after all, the ubiquitous white box has been the most popular form of decoration for the first 15 years of the 21st century. To some, this is a look of restraint and purity, but to others, it is cold, bland and sterile. Certainly walls recede when painted white and, because they reflect light, they make a room feel bigger. But white used in isolation does not necessarily create a relaxed atmosphere.

Using the carefully balanced shades of white and off-white, as outlined in the Neutrals section of this book (see pages 78–91), will prevent rooms from feeling lifeless while retaining a sense of continuity. Each neutral family, with its own personality and characteristics, can be used in any combination to create a flow throughout the house. The darkest tone could be chosen for the woodwork in one room, for the walls in the next and as an accent in a third. The lightest tone might be used on the floor in an area that lacks light and also on all the ceilings. The combinations possible with four colours are virtually endless, and you should feel confident in using them throughout the house to create a calm and cohesive look.

ONE CEILING COLOUR

Using the same colour for every ceiling in your home is a simple but effective way of creating flow. Although you may not even be aware that all the ceilings are painted the same tone, subconsciously the effect is both calming and comforting. This does not, however, mean that you should default to a bland and characterless white. Look at the lightest colour you have chosen for all the walls in your home – this often happens to be the wall colour chosen for the kitchen. If this colour is a white, it may well be that you could also use it on the ceiling and then continue with it on all the ceilings throughout the house.

If you choose stronger colours for your rooms, then a darker ceiling colour, such as 'Off-White', will serve to unite them.

THIS PAGE AND FACING PAGE
Although both the size of the rooms and the amount of natural light vary enormously throughout this Dutch house, the rooms are unified by all the wooden ceilings and beams being left unpainted. With high ceilings, you tend not to notice their colour very much, unlike lower ones, which become an integral part of the decorating scheme. Simple 'Strong White' has been chosen for all the walls.

ONE WOODWORK COLOUR

A single colour for all the woodwork throughout the house is seen by many as the easiest way to create a cohesive look. This could be one sympathetic white, as outlined on page 119. Indeed, it is often useful to have the same colour on both the ceilings and woodwork. The way a room is constructed however, may affect your choice of trim colour. If you have a traditional room with mouldings framing the doorways leading to other rooms, then the use of one colour on the trim forms a pleasing link that will create a visual bridge between each space. Many contemporary houses, with hardwood doors, have minimal amounts of trim, which makes the transition of colour from room to room through the use of one woodwork colour slightly trickier.

THIS PAGE AND FACING PAGE
All the owners of these houses have chosen a dark colour for their woodwork, but for different reasons. 'Down Pipe' on the skirting/baseboard and window frame (above left) creates a little extra drama. Glamorous 'Off-Black' gloss unifies the door and its frame (left) with all the others in the house. 'Railings', used on all the woodwork and on a little of the surrounding wall in this modish London apartment (facing page), makes the features look more expansive. Although these images are from different houses, you can imagine how using a dark colour on the trim throughout a property will create a seamless continuity.

FACING PAGE

Charlotte has chosen to make the hall of her West Country home the most decorative part of her house. Using flamboyant 'Lotus' (BP 2051) wallpaper on the walls, teamed with 'Teresa's Green' and 'Pointing', creates an exciting central scheme. Every room off the hall is artfully painted in tonally flowing colours, so all the spaces in the property are harmonious.

BELOW LEFT

All the colours in this house are tonally pleasing. One wall in the hall is 'Down Pipe', while the rooms off it are in colours from our Architectural Neutrals. The room in the foreground is in 'Blackened', the lightest of these.

BELOW RIGHT

The combination of 'Yeabridge Green' in the room nearest and 'Vardo' in the distance may cause some surprise at first. The scheme is certainly full of life but because the colours have the same tonal weight, it flows beautifully.

TONE-ON-TONE COLOUR

Colour can shift our focus and give us a visual destination, so it is often useful to work with colours that are connected tonally, in order to create the much sought-after sense of flow.

If you start with the strongest tone of a colour family, such as 'Pigeon', in a hallway, then use the slightly lighter 'Blue Gray' in the room beyond, and the even lighter 'Cromarty' in the room furthest away, this lighter room helps to achieve a greater sense of space.

BELOW LEFT
'Charlotte's Locks' in the hall
of this townhouse brings a
decorative excitement. Here,
we get an enticing glimpse of
it from a room painted in the
altogether calmer 'Teresa's
Green'. The spaces are united
by the 'Pointing' woodwork.

BELOW RIGHT
The 'Stone Blue' door is
an enticing invitation to
return to the adjacent hall.
But when entering the room,
painted in 'Buff' (A), you
pass this shot of colour
immediately and are less
aware of it once in the room.

FACING PAGE
It is an absolute delight
to stand in this neutral
hall and glimpse the
complementary colours
used in each of the three
bedrooms. 'Parma Gray',
'Calamine' and 'Dayroom
Yellow' sit perfectly
together and create a tingle
of anticipation before you
enter the individual rooms
and experience the different
colours close-up.

SEVERAL COLOURS

If you wish to unite different parts of the house with a cohesive look but still want to use a range of colours, then it is best to consider your colour choices floor by floor. In this way, you can envision how those colours in adjacent rooms will complement one another. If you stand in your hall, you can see into several rooms. If the relationship between these rooms is not taken into consideration, there will be no overall harmony.

The different colours used in the various rooms on the same floor should all have the same tonal weight. For example, sumptuous 'Hague Blue' in one room will sit harmoniously alongside the equally rich 'Card Room Green' and 'Eating Room Red', but it would feel far too heavy against fresh 'Green Ground' and delicate 'Middleton Pink'. To work in harmony with those shades, you would need to pick a much lighter, cleaner blue, such as 'Skylight', to create an equally weighted floor of rooms.

A UNIFYING HALL COLOUR

Halls can unify because they are visible from every room, so the colour of your hall is definitely the most important when it comes to maintaining a sense of flow and it is advisable to choose it before any of the other room colours. A hall's decorative scheme serves two purposes: to create an impression on arrival, setting the tone for the whole house, and, more importantly, to unite different parts of the house, making a smooth visual transition between rooms that might be decorated in a variety of styles and colours.

Mid-tone neutrals, such as 'Cornforth White' or 'Skimming Stone', are often used to achieve this. However, using a darker tone in the hall, such as 'Mole's Breath' or 'Charleston Gray', will not only spark interest and excitement on arrival, but will also make every room leading off it feel bigger and lighter, and leave you with at least five lighter neutrals to play with in all the other rooms. This may create almost imperceptible changes of colour, but these changes need to be there to create mood and sophistication.

There is, of course, always the option of choosing one accent colour and using it in different ways in every room. This works especially well if you also use the strong colour in your hall on a kitchen island, on the interior of a living room bookcase or on the underside of a bathtub. There are a million ways to introduce your accent colour into a room and by dint of this create a colour thread that leads throughout the house.

FACING PAGE
I am a great fan of the strong-coloured hall. Here, 'Down Pipe' is used as a central thread throughout the house. Although this colour may appear worryingly dark at first, remember that usually only a little amount of time is spent in the hall as you pass through the house. Such a strong central colour also gives you licence to be adventurous in other rooms.

ABOVE RIGHT
'Plummett' has been used on both the walls and woodwork in this diminutive hall,

creating a fabulous dramatic space and making every room off it appear bigger and lighter. It is interesting to see how the light makes the Estate Eggshell on the woodwork look so much lighter than the Estate Emulsion on the walls.

RIGHT
The owner of this elegant Paris apartment has chosen to use the wonderfully light-reflecting 'Tallow' on the walls in the hall, as well as on all the woodwork throughout the rest of the property, creating a natural flow through the space.

SHAPE &
FEATURE
WALLS

The very mention of a feature wall can strike horror in the hearts of some, while others will rub their hands with glee. Colour drastically adjusts our sense of space, and while large, awkward rooms can be helped by painting a single wall in a different colour to provide a focal point, a feature wall can just as easily destroy the proportions of a room if it is not executed correctly. A single wall painted in a bold colour can also bring life to a room, especially if the other colours are in sharp contrast, but it is important to understand how colours work together. Sharp contrasts are created by the use of complementary colours from the colour wheel (see pages 56–7), with each making the other look brighter and more intense. Colour is not only visually pleasing but a powerful tool for transforming spaces – it can certainly disguise awkward proportions, but remember that it can just as easily create them.

LEFT
Wow! 'Drawing Room Blue' and the starkly contrasting 'All White' above it make a bold statement and immediately make you want to explore this room. Painting an intense colour halfway up a wall where there is no dado rail is far easier to execute than you might imagine it, and is worth doing to create a stunning, individual look.

STRONG COLOUR ON A LONG WALL

If you use a bold colour on a longer wall with a lighter colour on the short walls, they will look as if they are being squeezed together, making the room appear longer and thinner. Colour on one long wall also makes for an uncomfortable room for sitting or sleeping in because the uneven nature of the space makes one feel all at sea. It is therefore advisable when creating a feature wall in a bedroom to put it behind the bedhead, thereby grounding the room and creating a pleasant atmosphere in which to wake up.

STRONG COLOUR ON A SHORT WALL

The use of a stronger colour on a shorter wall can make a room feel squarer in shape. Therefore, a long, thin room painted in 'Wevet', for example, with a bolder tone like 'Charlotte's Locks' used on a short wall, will foreshorten the space and help to create a more evenly proportioned room. Alternatively, a stronger colour can be used on the recesses on either side of a chimneybreast, to add depth while retaining balance.

ABOVE LEFT
Choosing sunny 'Babouche' for one wall in this slightly cramped bedroom means that the space immediately looks deeper, as well as injecting a delightful element of colour. The remaining walls and the ceiling are painted in a seamless 'Off-White' Estate Eggshell.

ABOVE RIGHT
'Off-Black' on a single wall of a child's bedroom in a Paris home creates both a focal and a talking point. Many children appreciate the security that a strong colour gives them, and this child is being introduced to a strong design ethic early.

ABOVE LEFT

Tucked into the eaves of a Scottish farmhouse, this charming guest room has been painted in 'Light Blue' so that the slightly compromised space feels bigger. 'Light Blue' has a magical quality, which makes it sometimes look blue and at other times grey.

LEFT

This lucky baby has had her nursery painted in 'Pelt', a colour that many people would shy away from when decorating for someone so young. However, the result is stunning and creates a wonderful cocoon-like space to grow up in.

ABOVE RIGHT

The window in this pretty bathroom is vast in proportion to the rest of the room, so the walls have been painted in 'Calamine', to warm up the space and make it feel a little more intimate. The glazed cupboard in 'Blue Ground' is a delightful contrast.

WARM AND COOL COLOURS

It is drummed into us that dark colours will always make a room look smaller. While there is an element of truth to this, it is much more useful to know that it is warm colours, like reds and yellows, that will make a room feel cosier because they appear to advance towards you. On the other hand, cool, bluer colours recede and, as a result, the space feels larger.

ABOVE

A seaside sitting room needs to feel airy and breezy, and this one certainly does just that. The huge amount of natural light, together with 'Parma Gray' on the walls and 'Wimborne White' on the woodwork, capitalizes on the available space and creates a room perfect for post-beach relaxation.

A STRONG CENTRAL COLOUR

Bold colour doesn't have to dominate, and combining colour with neutral tones can create striking schemes, as well as helping to change the sense of space in a room. If you use a darker colour in the centre of a room, everything around it will feel lighter and brighter. This technique is particularly successful when you paint a central kitchen island in a strong tone. If you don't have an island, you could paint the legs of a table in a darker tone instead, to ground the room, while keeping the strong colour well below eye level. The same can be said of painting the underside of, or the panelling around, a bathtub in a bright, neutral bathroom.

LARGE OR SMALL PATTERNS

Like so many things in decorating, it seems counterintuitive for a large pattern used in a small space to create an illusion of volume, and a small pattern to have a more enclosing effect, but they do. Therefore, wallpapers can be used to great effect to change the shape of a room. Intricate patterns, such as 'Renaissance Leaves' or 'Samphire', will immediately make a room feel cosy, while bigger, bolder patterns, such as 'Tessella' or 'St Antoine', lend a sense of grandeur and appear to enlarge a space.

ABOVE LEFT
Using the flamboyant damask 'St Antoine' (BP 953) (A) in this tiny bathroom was a wise choice, as it immediately makes the room feel bigger. Many people are wary of hanging art on a patterned background, but here you can see how my eclectic family portraits look totally at home.

ABOVE RIGHT
The delicate pattern of 'Yukutori' (BP 4304) wallpaper, inspired by Japanese pen-and-ink drawings of flying birds, is perfect for this kitchen. Although close-up you can appreciate the intricacy of each bird, as you move further away, the pattern becomes indistinct and serves purely to soften the walls.

FACING PAGE
I adore this room with its pared-down design ethic. The surprisingly strong wall colour, 'Dead Salmon', gives a warmth and glow to the space, while the outsized but simple kitchen island, painted in 'Railings', grounds the room, making everything around it feel lighter and bigger.

ACCENTS

Accent colours are usually introduced for the following reasons:

To add depth and balance
To enliven a drab space
To create a rhythm through the house

The joy of accent colours is that they can be used as boldly or as sparingly as you like. Those who are nervous about using them can introduce minute amounts of colour or pattern, which may well be hidden for 90 per cent of the time. Inside cupboards, on hidden sliding doors or on the underside of bathtubs, these pockets of colour will bring a smile to the face when they are occasionally revealed. Others like to make bold statements by painting strong colours on feature walls or chimneybreasts. But however brave you may feel, always remember that an accent colour should enhance rather than overwhelm the rest of your decorative scheme.

FACING PAGE
The simplicity of this
'Off-White' scheme is perfect
to show off both the graphic
poster and the two accent
chairs painted in 'Chinese
Blue' (A). The beauty of this
is that you can remove the
blue chairs when pining for
a totally neutral look or
even change the colour
according to the season.

ADDING DEPTH AND BALANCE

Even if you choose to live in the most understated of colour schemes, like those outlined in the Neutrals section of this book (see pages 78–91), a stronger accent of a similar tone can shift the balance of the room, thereby adding interest and impact. By including a deeper colour within the scheme, you will make the other colours in the neutral family come alive. The best accent colours for each family are as follows:

'Mouse's Back' with the Traditional Neutrals
'Mole's Breath' with the Easy Neutrals
'London Stone' with the Red-based Neutrals
'Cord' with the Yellow-based Neutrals
'Charleston Gray' with the Contemporary Neutrals
'Down Pipe' with the Architectural Neutrals

These accent colours can be incorporated in myriad ways, from entire walls to small pieces of furniture. For example, painting the joinery on either side of a chimneybreast in a darker tone creates depth and balance, but the bolder among you might choose to paint the chimneybreast itself in a stronger accent colour, which will also add an extra element to the decoration.

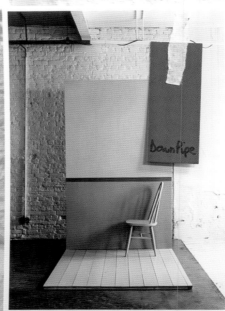

139

ENLIVENING A DRAB SPACE

If you are concerned that your decoration is a little plain, then using an accent colour in even the smallest of quantities can inject life into a colour scheme. The interiors of kitchen units, closets, and other hidden areas can be painted in uplifting colours to achieve an element of surprise without affecting the overall mood and style of the room.

Kitchen dressers come alive when the backs are painted in an accent colour, and, of course, the most effective way to display glass or china is against a dark colour. Another attraction of using a strong colour is that dark bookcases and shelving have a brilliant way of absorbing the clutter of everyday life. Historically, the use of accent colours in bookcases was quite common, either to enhance their contents or to add a little decorative flourish.

Nothing can lift the spirits more than opening a cupboard door and finding a sumptuous wallpaper on the interior, be it a closet for clothes, where damasks and pretty florals work perfectly, or a drinks cupboard, best suited to small patterns like 'Ocelot' or 'Samphire'. Children also delight in strong colours on the inside of their cupboards. They can choose these themselves, and for parents these choices remain hidden behind closed doors.

Whenever colour is used below the eye line it feels much less intimidating, so strong colour on the underside of freestanding bathtubs, kitchen islands and even on table legs is perfect if you are adverse to taking risks. Bold colours can go anywhere in the right dose, and a flamboyant accent colour on a piece of furniture that can be moved around a room is perfect for emphasis or contrast.

ABOVE RIGHT
Whenever you open the 'Yeabridge Green' cupboard door in this hall, which is painted the same colour, you cannot help but smile at the rich 'Yellow Ground' interior. The use of a single accent colour in all the cupboards throughout a house is a wonderful way of creating a rhythm and bringing a little joy into your life.

FACING PAGE
An intriguing dark paint effect has been used on the chimneybreast of this room, which adds an extra dimension. The strength of colour provides glamour and additional interest, particularly as it is combined with dusty 'Cinder Rose' on the walls. Both the wall colour and the paint effect stop at the picture rail, creating an intimate atmosphere.

140

THE MANUAL

CREATING A RHYTHM

Rhythm and flow in interior design come from repetition. You can use the same accent colour in different areas to encourage your eye to move around the room. The same technique can be adopted to create a visual bridge throughout a house. Consider painting your staircase in a darker accent colour, which will link all the floors of your house together and create a strong central spine, while taking on an almost sculptural quality. If you use the colour of the walls in one room as the accent colour in the next, you also create a pleasing link between the two.

Accent colours help define the mood of the room and can add a delightful flourish, but the relationship between colours and how they behave with each other is complex and requires careful balance. An accent colour should never dominate – it is there purely to add depth to the overall colour composition, and it should also make you smile.

FACING PAGE
As you enter this house, a fabulous graphic sign is a reminder of which city you are in. The strength of the sign is balanced by the staircase painted in 'Off-Black', which creates a satisfying dark spine for the house. The 'All White' panelling and 'Pavilion Gray' walls feel elegant and effortless in contrast to the accent stair colour.

ABOVE LEFT AND RIGHT
The joinery in both these bedrooms is identical, however the different accent wallpapers, which act almost as headboards, establish a very different character in each space. Confident 'Block Print Stripe' (BP 754) (left) is taken up the walls and over the top of the recess, to create a whimsical, almost tent-like feel, while glamorous 'Ocelot' (BP 3704) (right) has been reserved for just the back wall. Note how the vertical stripes make the space appear higher, while the more delicate pattern gives a feeling of width. Every bedroom in this French chateau features an accent wallpaper, thereby creating a pleasing link throughout the property.

ABOVE LEFT

By removing a couple of
cupboard doors, a witty desk
area has been created in
this teenager's bedroom.
The cupboards are painted in
'Brassica', although only up
to the height of the picture
rail in the rest of the room.
Brilliant 'St Giles Blue' has
been used as an accent in the
recess, to create a vibrant
and stimulating workspace.

ABOVE RIGHT

Papering the interior of
this cupboard in graphic
'Tourbillon' (BP 4807),
has given it a whole new
dimension. The segmented
circle pattern is fairly bold,
but when used in this way it
becomes far more understated.
If you are wary of pattern,
this is a great way to start
your journey to becoming a
lifelong wallpaper lover.

FACING PAGE

This bathroom is perfectly
balanced, with the five
colours therein artfully
combined to create a really
arresting but nevertheless
cohesive look. The quaint
blue bathtub and yellow
sanitaryware are the perfect
complement to the 'Hague
Blue' panelling, 'Pink
Ground' walls and 'Strong
White' floor.

FLOORS

———

There has long been a tradition of painting floors, and suddenly it is fashionable again. A couple of centuries ago, paint was used to imitate: wooden floors were painted to look like stone; stone flags to look like chequerboard; and ornate patterns created as an alternative to marquetry. These techniques can still be applied in the modern home, although floors are usually painted in a solid colour for a look that is both stylish and practical.

Farrow & Ball Floor Paint covers up a multitude of sins, bringing both old and new floors to life. Well-worn floors that have been patched with totally mismatching boards retain their character when painted, while cheap new boards gain a slight lustre that lends them a sense of permanence.

Every home contains rooms that would benefit from an easily washable floor covering. However, floor paint should be considered as much for its relaxed decorative qualities as for its durable ones. With Farrow & Ball Floor Paint available in every colour, it is easy to revamp the look of a room by simply painting the floor, and it is a lot less expensive than any other floor covering.

FACING PAGE
Both Charlotte and I find it
hard to resist painting at
least one feature in our
houses every week. Here,
she is updating her bathroom
with 'Brassica' Floor Paint.
It is as important to sample
Floor Paint as it is wall
paint, as colour can often
look totally different when
the light hits it from above.

PERSONAL STATEMENTS

While 'Shaded White' has been used on all the floorboards throughout this relaxed family home, huge visual interest has been added to the staircase by painting the risers 'Breakfast Room Green'. This is not only practical in defining the stairs, making them easier to use, but it can also disguise the scuff marks made by tiny feet. It also makes a bold personal statement that is decorative but not too overwhelming, as the use of strong colour below the eye line is relatively easy to live with.

IMAGINATIVE STRIPES

A combination of 'Brassica' and 'Manor House Gray' has been used on the floor in this relaxed sitting room, with a secretaire in one corner. The differing widths of the stripes are far from being a decorating mistake, as they define the various areas of the room. Despite understated 'Clunch' being used on the walls and woodwork, this particular look may be a little too anarchic for many. Floor paint is ever-flexible and allows the imagination to run wild.

WHITE AND LIGHT FLOORS

Kitchens are often very busy places, so using only one colour serves to bring a sense of calm to the space. Every element in this room is painted in the same colour, 'Slipper Satin', but the floor appears to be much lighter than the walls as the light flooding through the door is bounced around the room. Pale-coloured floors are the very best way to make the most of any available light.

STRONG-COLOURED FLOORS

Floor colour has a big impact on the look of a room, and the more floor space there is, the greater that impact. Be aware, a colour used on the floor will always look much lighter than the same tone on the walls. Here, bold 'India Yellow' on the floor of a simple white room acts as an anchor and also reflects a certain amount of the same shade onto the walls. It is the primary decorative statement in the room but it doesn't feel overwhelming as it so far below the eye line.

CONTINUITY IN FLOOR COLOUR

The owner of this room has used a variety of neutrals. 'Strong White' walls are teamed with 'Cornforth White' joinery. The lightest tone, 'Pointing', has been used on the floor, as in the rest of the house, resulting in a tranquil but modern-feeling scheme. Using the same colour on all the floors of a house is the perfect way to create a seamless flow.

CONTRASTING FLOOR COLOURS

'Mouse's Back', John Fowler's favourite carpet colour, has been used on the floor in the foreground, where its darker tone gives a solidity while remaining casual. The hall floor beyond is painted in 'Off-White', to bounce light onto the walls in this dark central space. Although using one colour throughout a house is best to ensure continuity, two contrasting floor colours, as shown here, can define spaces very effectively when there is a single wall colour.

SPLASHES OF COLOUR

In this house, decorated almost entirely in muted shades of white, it is a lovely surprise to come across this controlled dose of colour in the form of two simple 'Cook's Blue' stripes around the hearth. As well as drawing attention to the traditional tiles, they are a burst of something fun and modern, adding a personal feel to the room. Light bounces off the 'Clunch' floor and reflects onto the walls, creating the most charming atmosphere at any time of day.

DARK FLOORS

'Brassica' has been used on the floor in this relaxed space, with 'Drop Cloth' on the woodwork and 'Shadow White' on the walls. Despite its strength of colour, the floor does not dominate in the room. Using a darker colour on the floor than on the walls has in fact made the room look wider, maximizing the feeling of space.

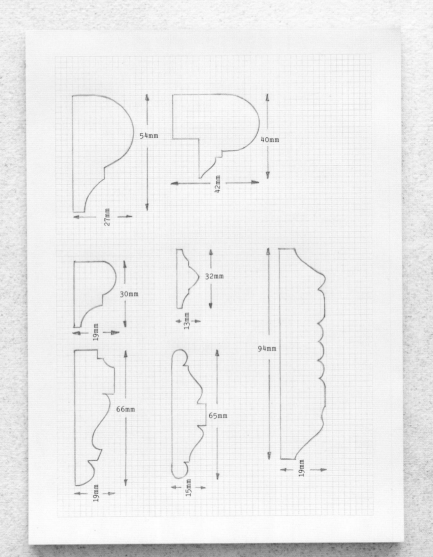

54mm

27mm

40mm

42mm

30mm

19mm

32mm

13mm

94mm

66mm

19mm

65mm

15mm

19mm

CHAIR &
PICTURE RAILS

It is important to remember that there are no hard-and-fast rules in decorating, and this is particularly true when it comes to the treatment of picture rails and chair rails. These architectural elements, and the walls around them, can be treated in many different ways, all of which will have a great effect on the overall appearance of your room.

Very often picture rails and chair rails are painted white through force of habit or, if the mouldings are particularly grand, to draw attention to their architectural beauty. Although there is nothing inherently wrong with this form of decorating, it does tend to create overly busy rooms. The eye is constantly drawn to the white stripes running around the room, rather than to the beautiful wall colour or the view.

Originally, these rails were painted to cover up mismatched wood grains and colours. They were purely functional parts of the architecture: chair rails to protect walls from furniture and picture rails for hanging paintings. There is, however, no practical reason why they should be picked out in a different colour from the wall, and it is only relatively recently that people have attempted to transform them into a feature, giving them misplaced importance and often making them the guiding decorative force.

In most contemporary rooms, the rails are either removed or simply painted the same colour as the walls for a strong, unified look. As there are no contrasts to distract the eye, this makes the room feel bigger.

CONTRAST OR HARMONY

If you decide to pick out your rails and make a feature of them, it is best to do it with the same white, or other colour, that you have used for the rest of the trim. Your preference may be for clean 'All White', which will create a fresh look with maximum contrast. Alternatively, you could try a tone that is more sympathetic to the wall colour (see Which White?, pages 96–7) for a more harmonious visual balance.

Having a chair rail gives you the opportunity to consider a range of options for the walls: two sympathetic paint colours, a combination of paint and wallpaper or two wallpapers – one above and one below the rail. Again, there are no rules about which area should be lighter or darker, but using a stronger colour above the chair rail than below can create a feeling of the walls tipping in towards you and the room closing in. Using a darker colour below the chair rail grounds the room and tends to make it open up and feel bigger. This is especially useful in long, thin entrance halls that are painted in neutrals. If you use a stronger tone, such as 'Charleston Gray', below the rail with the lighter 'Elephant's Breath' above, the hall will immediately feel wider and more airy.

Farrow & Ball makes combining paint colours and wallpaper especially easy. You can take the background or pattern colour of the wallpaper and paint this below the chair rail, with the corresponding paper above, or vice versa. It may be best to paint the chair rail the same colour as the wall below, to prevent the eye from being drawn to a white dividing line.

If the picture rail and the area of wall above it are painted the same colour as the rest of the wall, the ceiling will seem much higher. However, when the wall colour stops at the picture rail, the eye will be tricked into thinking that that is where the wall ends and the ceiling begins, visually lowering the ceiling. This can be useful in a very tall room, as you can bring the ceiling down to a more comfortable height, which will change the room's shape.

Another option to consider is to use gradation in colour. To achieve this, the main wall and picture rail should be the strongest colour, with a slightly lighter version above the picture rail and a sympathetic white on the cornice/crown moulding. This approach creates a feeling of transition up the wall and opens up a room, making it feel lighter and more spacious.

FACING PAGE TOP LEFT
The owner of this house has taken full advantage of the architectural elements of the room. By painting the wainscoting in 'Mole's Breath', a popular darker accent to accompany the Easy Neutrals group, and combining it with the much lighter 'Ammonite' on the walls, he has made the room feel larger and more airy.

FACING PAGE TOP RIGHT
The elegant panelling in this substantial Georgian drawing room is painted in timeless 'Off-White', while the walls are in the tonally perfect 'Light Gray'. Although using a darker colour above a lighter one can make a space feel smaller, when a room is this large, this classic approach works to perfection.

FACING PAGE BOTTOM LEFT
Using the same colour on both the walls and the panelling, a decorative trick much employed in the Georgian era, is extremely fashionable once more. Here, the uncertain black/blue tone of 'Railings' is suitably dramatic for this sensational Dutch home. Estate Emulsion on the walls and Estate Eggshell on the panelling result in a subtle variation in the level of sheen.

FACING PAGE BOTTOM RIGHT
The fact that the 'Stone Blue' on the walls in this country sitting room stops below the picture rail means that the perceived ceiling height lowers, making the room feel more intimate. The picture rail itself is painted in soft 'Lime White', as is all the other woodwork, while the wall above the rail and the ceiling are in the complementary lighter 'Slipper Satin'.

ABOVE LEFT
Although 'Hardwick White', seen here on the rustic tongue-and-groove panelling, is only a couple of shades darker than the 'Setting Plaster' on the walls, it still serves to ground the room and give it a warm and traditional feel.

ABOVE RIGHT
This basement corridor in a stately house, once used only by servants, now acts as the everyday entrance for the family. However, the original style of decoration has been preserved, with 'Dix Blue' Estate Eggshell painted onto the bottom half of the wall for extra durability. The scheme has been cleverly finished with a thin line of 'Off-Black' below the 'Pointing' walls.

FACING PAGE
This dining room contains every architectural element covered in this chapter. The wainscoting and the rail at the top of it have both been painted in 'Mole's Breath', with the skirting/baseboard in 'Strong White', in order to be consistent with the rest of the room. 'Ammonite' on the walls and above the picture rail makes the 'Strong White' ceiling feel higher.

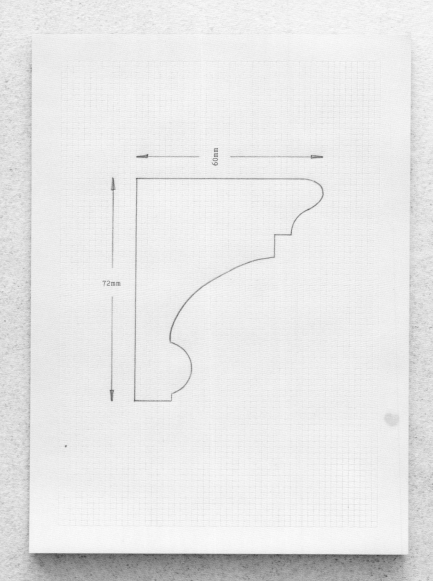

CORNICING
& MOULDING

Who could imagine that a seemingly insignificant piece of plaster moulding could change the shape, height and style of a room to such a degree? Most people don't give it much thought, but I can assure you that these architectural mouldings can completely transform your space if painted the appropriate colour.

First, I should point out that the mouldings have different names on either side of the Atlantic. In Britain, we refer to them as cornice, or coving, while in the US they are usually called crown moulding. The origin of both terms is classical, from the Latin *coronis* and the Greek *koronis*, meaning crown. Whichever term you use, I am referring to the decorative element that runs around the top of a room to cover the transition from wall to ceiling.

Embellished cornices/crown mouldings tend to be used in larger, more ornate interiors and are to be treasured. The plainer type are generally used in simpler, contemporary homes. However, both can be painted in four basic ways:

Moulding and ceiling the same colour
Moulding and walls the same colour
Gradating colour from walls to ceiling
Picking out the moulding in an accent colour

This uncomplicated scheme uses 'Wimborne White' on both the ceiling and moulding, which is a popular decorative technique. The soft nature of 'Wimborne White' sets off the gentle tone of 'Shaded White' on the walls.

Crisp 'All White' has been extended over the ceiling and down onto the moulding in this smart study, where there is ample ceiling height. This is the perfect choice because the moulding hits the top of the window

architrave, also painted in 'All White', preventing a mean strip of wall colour above the frame. The walls are painted in 'Parma Gray'.

This moulding is designed so that it extends onto the ceiling, making it inappropriate to paint it anything but the ceiling colour — in this case, 'James White', which complements the 'Lime White' walls.

MOULDING AND CEILING THE SAME COLOUR

Very often the moulding and ceiling are painted the same plain white, either out of habit or a wish for clean simplicity. However, this does tend to make the perceived height of the room drop by the depth of the moulding. This is because we register the top of the wall at the point where it meets the white of the moulding, making the wall appear shorter than it actually is. Matching the moulding and ceiling is most appropriate when the protruding part of the moulding, which sits on the ceiling, is bigger than the dropping part, which sits against the wall. In this case, it would look clumsy to have anything but the ceiling colour on the moulding.

MOULDING AND WALLS THE SAME COLOUR

Painting the moulding the same colour as the walls will make the walls appear taller and the room feel loftier. This approach is particularly effective if you are using plain convex moulding, purely as a means to soften the transition from wall to ceiling. Using the same colour on the walls and mouldings also gives a simple and strong, contemporary feel to a room.

GRADATING COLOUR FROM WALLS TO CEILING

Many people want to draw attention to their moulding, and if a subtle gradation of colour is used between the walls and the ceiling, it can create a visual balance in the room. If you are using a very strong colour on the walls, it may feel uncomfortable to use the same tone on the moulding. In this case, it is best to consider a gradation of colour. Not only will this make the room feel higher, but the eye will be led gently upwards, rather than being pulled dramatically towards the ceiling.

If the wall is painted a strong red, then consider using warm 'Joa's White' on the moulding, to bridge the gap between the wall colour and the ceiling colour. Contemporary 'Mole's Breath' on the walls would call for 'Ammonite' on the moulding, and sunny 'Yellow Ground' would be best matched with 'House White'. Fortunately, for every Farrow & Ball colour, there is a sympathetic white (see pages 96–7), which can ease the transition between wall and ceiling and contribute to the harmony of a room.

PICK OUT THE MOULDING IN AN ACCENT COLOUR

Painting the moulding in a colour that contrasts with the walls and the ceiling creates a crisp, tailored room. However, because your eye will be naturally drawn to a strong contrast, it often means that you are constantly reading the shape and confines of the room, which makes it feel smaller overall. Highly coloured moulding tends to be for the very adventurous, but the use of a subtle tone, such as 'Dove Tale', against a 'Skimming Stone' wall, or 'Worsted' with 'Shadow White', provides a decorative touch that gives character and distinction without ruining the room's proportions. It is essential that the ceiling is painted in a sympathetic tone.

This method of decoration is most often used when one wants to draw the eye to both the decorative moulding and a ceiling rose, which should be painted in the same colour.

All too often, decorative mouldings, including ceiling roses, have been painted over so many times that they end up losing a lot of their delicate detail. In order to prevent this from happening on intricate moulding, and to create a really traditional, authentic look, it makes sense to use a specialist finish such as Soft Distemper or Limewash, provided that the moulding has not previously been painted with an emulsion.

CEILINGS

Very little thought is usually given to the colour of the humble ceiling. However, it causes more controversy than any other subject in decorating. Although ceilings are so often painted in some ubiquitous colourless paint, there is no rule to say that they have to be white. Ceiling colour affects a room in different ways, so in the next section we cover the following topics:

Making a room look lighter or darker
Changing a room's perceived height
Same colour for ceilings and walls

Consider the ceiling to be your fifth wall and give it due consideration – its colour is absolutely vital to your overall decorative scheme. And don't forget that the use of Full Gloss on the ceiling has an amazing effect on a room, as does the application of wallpaper, if you are feeling very brave.

FACING PAGE
The ornamental ceiling is just one of the exquisite decorative features in this enviable hall. Sometimes a very simple colour, such as 'Wimborne White' used here, is all that is needed. The magnificent architecture and superb light do the rest. Casein Distemper has been used to enhance the stunning detail.

BELOW RIGHT
The pronounced differentiation between the 'Pitch Black' feature wall and the 'All White' ceiling instantly draws the eye to the point where they meet. This works to great effect in such a striking room, but elsewhere it could make the ceiling look lower by drawing attention to the top of the wall.

FACING PAGE
Had the wooden ceiling of this Scottish breakfast room been painted a bright white, the room would not be nearly as appealing and the walls would have looked so much darker. The 'Off-White' ceiling sits perfectly atop the 'Blue Gray' walls, softening the junction where the two meet.

MAKING A ROOM LOOK LIGHTER OR DARKER

Most of us grew up with the fixed notion that it is definitely advantageous to make ceilings as light and bright as possible. However, using a bright white can actually make a room feel considerably darker. This may sound counterintuitive, but it isn't if you remember that decorating with colour is all about contrast. The lighter the colour is on the ceiling, the darker the walls will appear. A bright white will make even the subtlest of colours feel relatively dark. To prevent this, it is advisable to use a white that is sympathetic to the wall colour, resulting in a lighter, more cohesive room. To help you choose the best whites to accompany each colour, see pages 96–7.

CHANGING A ROOM'S PERCEIVED HEIGHT

If you use a bright white on the ceiling with coloured walls, the contrast between the two is so great that one's eye is immediately drawn upwards, to read where the wall ends and the ceiling begins. Having read the top edge of the walls, you are immediately aware of the ceiling height, which causes it to drop.

If, however, you choose a white for the ceiling that is more sympathetic to the tone on the walls, it will feel as if the wall colour has just gradated into a lighter tone on the ceiling. You are then much less aware of where the walls end and the ceiling begins, which means that the perceived ceiling height will rise. Old-school decorators would very often mix 25 per cent of the wall colour into the ceiling white to achieve this effect. Luckily, Farrow & Ball have done all this work for you – there is a sympathetic white, with the correct coloured undertone, for every wall colour in our palette.

It is also worth noting that if you have a very high ceiling and want to bring it down to a more comfortable height, then you should use a darker tone on the ceiling than on the walls. This will visually lower the height of a space and make it more intimate.

SAME COLOUR FOR CEILING AND WALLS

Using the same colour on the ceiling as on the walls creates a soothing atmosphere. With both planes the same colour, it is difficult to tell where the walls end and the ceiling begins, which results in the perceived ceiling height rising and, at the same time, creating a rich atmosphere that feels just right and not at all overwhelming.

This approach is particularly effective when there is no cornice, or crown moulding, and you don't wish to draw attention to the point where the walls and ceiling meet. A continuous field of colour covers up a multitude of sins, and you can camouflage an oddly angled ceiling by taking the colour up the wall and over the ceiling.

ABOVE LEFT
The brave decision to take 'Stiffkey Blue' wall colour onto the ceiling turns the naturally darker end of this room into an intimate, inviting space. It also creates a definite delineation from the lighter kitchen area painted in 'Wimborne White'.

ABOVE RIGHT
'Lulworth Blue' has been used on the walls and ceiling, resulting in a charming and gently enveloping room. Using only one colour means that the fresh white bed linen stands out to great effect.

FACING PAGE
Although one might be wary of creating a sense of claustrophobia by painting the ceiling a strong colour, it is the perfect solution for this slightly compromised area. Both the walls and ceiling have been painted in 'Mole's Breath', making it difficult to read the confines of the space.

FACING PAGE
'Cabbage White', on both
the walls and ceiling, has
transformed this tiny attic
space into the most desirable
bedroom. Although the room
still feels intimate, all the
planes have been painted
the same colour, which
increases the sense of space.

ABOVE LEFT
The quirky nature of this
room's architecture has been
embraced. Instead of trying
to hide the sloping ceiling,
it has been adorned with wide
stripes of 'Mouse's Back',
'Lulworth Blue' and 'Red
Earth', each complementing
the hue of its neighbour.

ABOVE RIGHT
Winsome 'Uppark' (BP 523)
wallpaper decorates the walls
and pitched ceiling of this
diminutive attic bedroom.
This approach makes the
ceiling seem higher. 'All
White', the colour of the
wallpaper pattern, features
on the flat ceiling.

CHILDREN'S BEDROOMS

The decoration of children's bedrooms is often the source of considerable angst – the age-old dilemma of whether to keep to the established colour-flow of the rest of the house or to allow the child free rein will never go away. There are, however, many ways around it, which should please both the parent and the child. Over the next few pages, we cover some understated and practical solutions, as well as some that are more adventurous.

Using small areas of strong colour alongside neutrals often satisfies both parties. The simplest approach is to use a strong colour on the woodwork and a lighter tone on the walls. Choose a neutral colour sympathetic to your established colour palette for the walls and then indulge in some bold colour for the skirting/baseboard and doors. 'Hague Blue' woodwork with 'Blackened' walls is the perfect scheme for the modern child, or swap 'Blackened' for 'Skylight' for a more classic look, evocative of the seaside. If you are resistant to pink for a child's room, then delicate 'Pale Powder', which is neither blue nor green, works fantastically well teamed with 'Green Blue' woodwork. For a more neutral room, try 'Great White' on the walls and 'Brassica' on the trim.

FACING PAGE

Soft aquas are firm favourites for children's bedrooms because the green undertone prevents a room from ever feeling cold. 'Dix Blue' has been used on this adventurous, high-level bed and the wall behind it. A ladder in exhilarating 'Yellowcake' generates a little more excitement but without being overpowering.

All children's schemes can be enhanced by introducing a bold colour on storage units, beds or other furniture. It's the same as when using a strong colour on a central kitchen island: by placing a darker object in a room, everything around it will look lighter.

If you are wary of colour, then painting a stronger hue in a recess or the interior of cupboards or bookshelves is most effective. The child can be given the opportunity to choose the colour themselves and, of course, it can be changed very easily as they grow in age and sophistication.

Fun wallpaper lining a cupboard helps to start the day well, and is a discreet decorative touch as it is not in view at all times. Bold designs include 'Closet Stripe' and 'Tented Stripe', while the more delicate 'Yukutori', with its soft outline of birds, and the charming 'Bumble Bee', a Farrow & Ball favourite, are equally appealing.

Coloured ceilings seem to thrill most children and shouldn't be restricted just to the obvious blue, or, indeed, to paint. On entering a neutral room with a coloured ceiling, it takes a moment before you become aware of it, which introduces an element of surprise. Even the merest wash of colour on the ceiling will infuse a space with a little individuality.

Full Gloss on ceilings make them glint and shine, creating a jewel-like quality. Alternatively, if you want to really indulge your child, consider 'Brockhampton Star' or 'Vermicelli' wallpapers on the ceiling. Their metallic patterns will catch the light and create a twinkling treat overhead.

Painted stripes, either horizontal or vertical, are a great favourite with children of all ages. When created in bold colours, such as 'Charlotte's Locks' and 'Pelt', they have a graphic edge more

suitable for teenagers. Or if you prefer a calmer and more tranquil look, paint stripes in sympathetic neutrals or even in the same colour as the walls but in a different finish.

Spots, targets, flowers and other graphic shapes are all relatively simple to paint directly onto the wall. What's more, they're the perfect use for sample pots.

However you introduce colour, or, indeed, if you would prefer a stylish but more subdued room for your child, it is fun for both of you if they are involved. Many children have an inventive and idiosyncratic approach to using colour, which helps to create spaces that reflect their personality and individuality. It doesn't have to be a riot of colour, but hopefully you can sign them up early to be a lifelong Farrow & Ball fan.

ABOVE LEFT
The lucky twins in this bedroom have an exciting combination of blues. The walls are painted in 'Stone Blue', with an intriguing 'St Giles Blue' stripe around the room. Each child chose a blue for the painted headboard, defining the position of their vintage iron beds: 'Hague Blue' for the boy, 'Parma Gray' for the girl.

ABOVE RIGHT
The little girl in this bedroom had her dreams answered in the shape of gentle 'Middleton Pink' decoration. The purest of the Farrow & Ball pinks, it has a delicate feel but rarely looks overwhelmingly sugary. The dark door from the hall provides an unexpected dramatic entrance.

FACING PAGE
Many a moody teenager has yearned for a black bedroom, much to the horror of their parents. The slightly lighter 'Down Pipe' painted on these walls satisfies the urge to move to the dark side while remaining super-stylish.

The lucky occupant of this room has the privilege of being bathed in glorious light from two directions. Wisely, the walls have been left totally neutral, painted in 'White Tie', a slightly yellowed white that will enhance the sunny, upbeat feel of the space.

Hedgerow-inspired
'Hornbeam' wallpaper
has been presented in
two different colourways
in this charming room.
The juxtaposition of the
stronger-coloured paper
with its 'Red Earth' pattern
below the dado rail, and the
lighter paper above, grounds
the room and makes it feel
bigger, while giving an
unexpected decorative twist.

WALLPAPER

Choosing wallpaper is extremely personal. Whether you want to make a big, bold statement or just create a little texture on the wall, Farrow & Ball has a wallpaper to suit. There is a wealth of choice, from the flamboyant 'Bamboo' to the mellow 'Silvergate', as illustrated over the next few pages, where the images show examples of how to use papers in different ways and in order to make the most of their particular qualities.

Using metallic papers to bounce light around a room
(see above right on page 188)
Combining two papers together to make a room look larger
(see facing page)
Using subtle pattern to create interest on very flat walls
(see above left on page 188)
Using traditional and modern wallpaper designs to enhance your home *(see pages 186, 187 and above left on page 189)*
How easy it is to combine Farrow & Ball wallpaper and paint together *(see page 190)*
How to use wallpaper to make you smile, whether it be on a feature wall or a headboard *(see below right on page 191)*

If you are tempted to break into pattern but wary of the commitment, remember to start small – the interiors of cupboards and small bathrooms are crying out for wallpaper. Or use a flamboyant pattern in a room that isn't frequented every day, perhaps a dining room or a guest bedroom. You will be in for a real treat when you do use these spaces, or even just catch a glimpse of fabulous pattern as you pass by an open door.

LEFT
Deep red 'Feuille' (BP 4904) wallpaper makes for a warm and welcoming traditional kitchen. Its classic pattern, like a damask but with more fluidity, has an almost velvety appearance, introducing equal amounts of drama and informality — informal enough for an invasion of chickens.

FACING PAGE
Although very on trend, this whispering 'Feather Grass' (BP 5102) wallpaper makes you feel as if you are at one with nature, in the middle of a meadow. What better way could there be to escape the stresses of modern life?

ABOVE LEFT
The fragile pattern
and delicate colourway
of 'Blostma' (BP 5203)
wallpaper bring a tender,
nurturing atmosphere to this
apartment, which overlooks
a park. Like many Farrow &
Ball wallpapers, the pattern
becomes less distinct from
a distance, serving just to
soften the walls and make
them feel less flat.

ABOVE RIGHT
This 'Bumble Bee' (BP 547)
wallpaper, which has
long been a Farrow &
Ball classic, was inspired by the
silk fabric in Joséphine
Bonaparte's bed chamber.
Often used in the stronger
colourways for light-starved
cloakrooms, it is also a
favourite in children's
bedrooms. It seems a natural
choice for this room in a
French chateau, where the
doors have been painted to
complement the metallic
repeat in the paper.

ABOVE LEFT
For many, this 'Bamboo'
(BP 2119) wallpaper brings
back memories of the 1970s.
Whether used ironically or
as a life-affirming decorative
tool, as in this child's
room, it always serves to
raise the height of the room,
in much the same way as a
vertical stripe does.

ABOVE RIGHT
It would be hard to find a
prettier or more soothing
bathroom. The English
damask 'Silvergate' (BP 804)
covers the walls, with
the corresponding neutral
'Pointing' on the woodwork
and the underside of the
bathtub. The equally
colourless linen curtains
add to the calm vibe.

The beauty of using a
Farrow & Ball wallpaper,
such as the glorious 'Lotus'
(BP 2051) shown in this hall,
is that you can have complete
confidence that there will be
paint colours to work with it
perfectly. 'Teresa's Green',
the colour of the pattern,
has been painted on the dado
area below the rail, while
'Pointing' has been used on
the woodwork, creating a
totally seamless design.

BELOW LEFT

With its abundant, trailing
design of blossoming flowers,
this 'Wisteria' (BP 2212)
wallpaper, a classic
19th-century English floral
pattern, is incredibly
romantic and results in rooms
that have a certain flourish.
It has been used here in the
bedroom of a French chateau.
Amazingly, the upholstered
chair sits perfectly with
the unusual grey and
yellow colourway.

BELOW RIGHT

Over the years, Charlotte
and I have been a tad
competitive in our
decorating. I am very
enthusiastic about painting
headboards directly onto
walls, but, of course, she
went one step further,
creating this spectacular
scalloped creation out of
our 'Silvergate' (BP 852)
damask wallpaper.

EXTERIORS

Exterior colour not only makes a property appealing from the street but it also sets the tone for the whole house. Whether you have a cottage or a castle, a contemporary or classic building, there are many ways to introduce colour to exteriors. All of the exterior – masonry, walls, window frames, ironwork, planters and the front door – may need to be painted and should be considered as a whole, just as you would the architectural elements in a room.

As with interiors, when it comes to choosing colours, there are no rights or wrongs, but it is best to take into account certain factors such as the location of your property, as described on the following pages.

FACING PAGE

I am not sure which is the more appealing, the enchanting garden door painted in 'Brassica' Exterior Eggshell or the furry hound who lives here. The walls are in 'Joa's White' Masonry Paint, to give the impression of warmth.

ASPECT OF YOUR HOME & SURROUNDING AREA

When decorating the exterior of your home, you can afford to consider a shade that is darker than you might choose for the interior, because the light conditions are so different. If, for example, you are considering 'Ammonite', try the stronger 'Purbeck Stone', or 'Pigeon' instead of 'Blue Gray'.

It certainly makes sense to choose colours that suit the environment, and it is always best to look at possible colours in situ. Vibrant tones that might seem perfect in the bright sunshine of the Caribbean will look nothing but garish in northern light.

Similarly, the subtle tones of a crofter's cottage will appear lifeless in bright sunshine. Dominant features like brickwork, natural wood and other expanses of colours, such as paved or gravelled areas, lawns, fencing, shrubs and even flowers, should also be taken into account, as they all affect colour choice.

In a rural setting you may want the house to recede into the landscape. In this case, muted, green-based tones like 'Old White' or 'Lime White' work best on masonry, with sympathetic 'Slipper Satin' on the woodwork to minimize contrasts. For a mellow, sophisticated look, paint any planters and benches sitting against the house in one from the large selection of stone colours: 'Oxford Stone' for a warm look, 'Fawn' for a greener feel or 'String' for an understated yellower scheme.

In urban settings it is more important to be sensitive to the style and colour of neighbouring buildings, and decide whether you want a complementary or contrasting scheme. If the entire street has white trim, it may be wise to follow suit – even the subtlest off-white could look dirty against bright white on an adjacent building. For this reason, charcoal-greys like 'Down Pipe' are now popular on exterior trim because they stand out from the crowd.

THE PERIOD OF YOUR PROPERTY

The architectural style of your property, and the period in which it was built is certainly more relevant when it comes to painting the exterior than the interior. Elegant Regency houses need only neutrals on their stucco facades and equally understated colour on their front doors, while Victorian houses can definitely sustain stronger colours.

Using bold colour on the outside of urban buildings has become very popular. A really strong exterior not only creates the ultimate impact, but also makes the interior feel lighter on entry.

The colour families outlined in the Neutrals section of this book (see pages 78–91) can be layered on exteriors, to enhance or detract from the architecture, just as you would do in an interior. The darkest tone should be used on the masonry with a mid-tone on the brickwork and the lightest tone on windows and frames. However, do not use more than three colours on the exterior, otherwise it begins to look messy.

It is a good idea to paint the front door and any other neighbouring woodwork, such as garage doors, window boxes and garden gates, in the same colour. There are two finishes to choose from: Full Gloss on the door, for gravitas, and the slightly more relaxed-looking Exterior Eggshell on everything else.

FACING PAGE
'Down Pipe' has been chosen for all the exterior woodwork of this early 18th-century house. A dark charcoal colour when used for interiors, 'Down Pipe' appears somewhat softer when painted on the outside. The fact that the doorframe is the same colour as the door itself makes the house appear much more imposing.

RIGHT
This attractive clapboard house in a Dulwich terrace, London, has been given a modern twist by painting both the masonry and the woodwork in the same colour: 'Off-Black'. This creates a strong, confident look that is somewhat tempered by the 'Blue Ground' on the front door. White on the picket fence and struts brightens the overall effect.

CONNECTING INTERIOR & EXTERIOR

Using the same colour on the exterior and interior of a house
creates a seamless continuity and often makes rooms feel bigger.
To create this flow, take the wall colour of a room, however vibrant,
and use it on a flowerpot or bench in the garden, to visually connect
the two spaces. If the same colour is chosen for both exterior and
interior window frames, this helps to blur the distinction between
the house and garden. Of course, if the window frames are also
painted the same colour as the walls, you will instantly feel more
connected to your outside space.

FACING PAGE
Six front doors of very different styles and painted in an assortment of colours. Intense 'Pitch Blue' (top left), striking 'Yellowcake' (top middle), full-blooded 'Incarnadine' (top right), peaceful 'Oval Room Blue' (bottom left), warming 'Brassica' (bottom middle)

and classic 'All White' (bottom right). Which colour would you choose?

BELOW LEFT
The shepherd's hut is considered one of the most romantic dwellings. The simplicity of the exterior and the cosy shelter it can provide are a heady mix.

This renovated beauty has been painted in 'Blue Gray' on the outside, a colour that sits perfectly within the landscape, while the inside is fresh 'Wimborne White'.

BELOW RIGHT
Planning regulations prevented this astonishing west London house from being

built with more than one storey, so it was designed to be partially below street level. Although the paintwork was originally intended to be kept in the architect's white, the new owners have added their own splash of colour by painting the garden walls in a mix of 'Card Room Green' and 'Down Pipe'.

TREATING THE ENTRANCE

The eye will always look for a focal point and you can use colour to help you make one. To make a feature of your home's entrance, paint the front door and its complete frame in one colour – this will make it look bigger and more imposing. Consider the paint finish as well as the colour for your front door. Exterior Eggshell creates a relaxed feel in soft colours and a more contemporary look in strong colours. Full Gloss, meanwhile, gives a classic, more traditional look and is especially effective in strong colours such as 'Hague Blue', 'Black Blue' or 'Railings', which look both chic and discreet.

Colour used outside can have a truly transformative effect. Whether you want to complement pale honeyed stonework with modest shades, disguise a house clad in weatherboarding or make a stunning backdrop for plants and foliage, don't forget to always work with your architectural elements as well as with nature. The colour of guttering or downpipes should be chosen to complement the lead on a building, just as the colour of a bench under a fabulous blossom tree should be selected to enhance the shade of the flowers.

ABOVE LEFT
The impressive doors of this byre were the inspiration for 'Inchyra Blue'. This strong colour creates a dramatic entrance, while sitting perfectly beneath the expansive Scottish skies.

ABOVE RIGHT
Alongside its larger neighbour (see left), this little gem of a play house has been painted in 'Railings', with 'Slipper Satin' on the windows, door and roof decoration. It is a design that is enjoyed by the occasional small occupants and their parents alike.

ABOVE LEFT
This charming stone farmhouse is a picture of rural bliss. The stone itself contains a million different colours, all of which could have been the starting point for the choice of colour on the front door. The uncertain nature of 'Green Blue' does the job perfectly, complementing the stone, as well as making a very welcoming entrance.

ABOVE RIGHT
'Mizzle', the colour inspired by a mix of mist and drizzle, has been used on the exterior of this American clapboard house. Inside, 'Mizzle' has a definite blue tone, but outside the blue virtually disappears and it looks like a soft, weathered grey.

ERAS

If you are nostalgic for the past, you may want to source authentic colours for your home. Of course, it is important to look at the features of your building and take the date of your house into account. However, it is a grave mistake to pressurize yourself into using only colours that are historically correct.

Our houses are not archaeological sites, to be painted in painstakingly re-created original colour schemes. Better to remember that they are our homes to be lived in and enjoyed in the 21st century, regardless of when they were built. By all means, respect the colours of the past, but don't be a slave to them – many historically accurate palettes can lead to either dreary and oppressive rooms or spaces that are so full of colour they are too demanding to live in.

The joy of colour is that it has developed over the years, and we should embrace this, together with the changes that have taken place in our buildings – we now have bigger windows than ever before and definitely better lighting. The Farrow & Ball palette has been designed with this in mind, so the colours seem both ageless and up to the minute. They are perfect interpretations of true period colours.

The following pages give a broad outline of the type of colours used in the four main decorative periods:

Georgian
Victorian
Edwardian
Art Deco & Mid-Century

GEORGIAN

'Off-White'

'Lichen'

'Mouse's Back'

'Picture Gallery Red'

The Georgian period is often referred to as the Age of Elegance. During this time the rooms of the well-to-do were usually of the most exacting proportions – the perfect backdrop for the carefully balanced mix of colours that are a signature of this age, and so perfect for the Farrow & Ball palette.

Decoration was a major indicator of wealth and status, so decorative plasterwork and stucco were much in evidence, as was panelling, all of which were usually coloured in tones like 'Lime White', 'Off-White' or even 'Fawn'. Paint became particularly important with the use of softwood in the home; cheap and versatile, but not durable, it needed to be painted.

Iron and red oxides were the cheapest and most commonly used pigments at this time, creating colours like 'Mouse's Back' and 'Dead Salmon' – two Farrow & Ball classics. Early Georgian colour schemes would also have included colours like 'Lichen', 'Pigeon' and 'Picture Gallery Red', all of which would generally have been used with a sheen akin to Estate Eggshell.

In the Regency period, colours became lighter, with dusky pinks like 'Setting Plaster', soft greys like 'Pavilion Gray', and cleaner greens and blues like 'Breakfast Room Green' and 'Lulworth Blue', as well as strong yellows like 'Straw' (A). These would have been used in a matt finish like Dead Flat or Estate Emulsion.

VICTORIAN

'Citron'

'Joa's White'

'Eating Room Red'

'Parma Gray'

Victorian interior design ideas were the result of the era being one of great change. Homes were upgraded quickly due to mass production, so decoration in this period had a somewhat cluttered and heavy look, summed up by the use of dark brown paint on woodwork, which was so beloved by the Victorians.

At the start of the Victorian period, lighter warm tones like 'Dimity' and 'Calluna' were still fashionable, along with iridescent whites such as 'Great White'. However, darker reds like 'Eating Room Red' and 'Brinjal' remained popular in masculine dining rooms and libraries, teamed with a warm white like 'Joa's White' on the ornate plasterwork, resulting in a rich, sumptuous interior.

As time moved on, these colours were superseded by a much stronger, cleaner palette dominated by crisp blues like 'Parma Gray', rich greens like 'Calke Green' and solar yellows such as 'Citron'. By the end of the 19th century, colours were once again more muted and soft, best represented by 'Cinder Rose' and 'Green Smoke'.

From the 1840s, wallpaper was in mass production and often installed from the skirting/baseboard up to the dado rail or even sometimes to the picture rail. By the middle of the Victorian period, heavily patterned wallpapers (and flocks) were seen in most houses. The background colours to these papers were usually fairly drab, like 'French Gray' or 'London Stone'.

EDWARDIAN

'Skylight'

'Ringwold Ground'

'Wimborne White'

'Cooking Apple Green'

Edwardian style was seen as a breath of fresh air after the heaviness, clutter and dark colours of Victorian interiors. People wanted something less formal, so rails and panelling began to disappear from homes, and there were fewer but larger rooms, with an increased amount of natural light. There was also a return to a simpler, more pared-down approach to colour.

Pastel blue tones like 'Skylight' and 'Pale Powder', fresh greens like 'Tunsgate Green' and 'Green Ground', and pinks such as 'Calamine' were all used to create a sense of space. Simple creams like 'Tallow' and 'Ringwold Ground' were also much in evidence.

However, in dining rooms, richer hues like 'Dorset Cream' continued to be used, and details were still highlighted in strong colours. For example, woodwork might be painted in a colour close to 'Tanner's Brown'.

Wallpaper patterns were feminine, with floral designs often featured to represent the Edwardian ideal of freshness and light.

Woodwork, cornices/crown mouldings and ceilings were painted using the new bright white paint akin to 'All White' or 'Wimborne White'. 'James White' or 'Pointing' could also be used to promote the light, uncomplicated feel that became so important during this post-Victorian era.

ART DECO & MID-CENTURY

'Churlish Green'

'Shaded White'

'Black Blue'

'Babouche'
(centre)

Art Deco interior design originated in Europe and by the end of World War I it was the leading decorating style, characterized by rich colours, bold geometric shapes and lavish ornamentation.

The most popular colours were strong and uncompromising. Black was often used, either 'Pitch Black' or 'Black Blue', and usually in gloss, to complement all the chrome. Strong yellows like 'Babouche' also featured, along with clean reds like 'Incarnadine' and 'Blazer'. These were often combined with a grey on the woodwork, either cool 'Blackened' or stronger 'Down Pipe', emphasizing the angular shapes of this era. Geometric wallpapers were incredibly popular. Although not strictly from this period, 'Tessella', 'Ranelagh' and all the striped wallpapers could be used to represent this time, as long as they are in strong colours.

By the mid-century, decor had become even crisper and more uncluttered. Creams and neutrals like 'Shaded White' and 'Skimming Stone' accompanied vibrant greens like 'Yeabridge Green', 'Churlish Green' or even playful 'Arsenic'. No list of mid-century colours would be complete without mentioning a saturated blue-green like 'Teresa's Green' or the earthier 'India Yellow', often teamed with the deep tones of 'London Clay' to give the illusion of architectural detail in an otherwise plain room.

HOW TO PAINT

If you plan to do the decorating yourself, the task in hand can feel a little overwhelming. The following tips, along with an outline of essential items (see pages 212-13) and an easy-to-calculate coverage table (see page 98), are designed to make the job a little easier. You are about to transform your home, and the process should be fun.

1

Clear as much as you can from the room or cover it with dust sheets. Use masking tape, which won't damage any surfaces, to cover light switches and plug sockets. Tape around the edges of the trim to protect it from the wall colour. If you have carpet, mask around the carpet edge to make painting the trim easier and reduce the risk of carpet fibres getting onto the freshly painted surface.

2

It is useful to gather all your tools and materials together in one place for easy accessibility. You will need a stick to stir your paint to ensure it is properly mixed, and some good-quality brushes and rollers. These are an invaluable investment because they don't leave brushmarks or an orange-peel texture on the walls. Keep a damp cloth or rag to hand to mop up any spills.

3

Professional painters will always spend more time prepping than actually painting. This is the boring bit, but the more care you take at this stage, the better the paint will look and the longer it will last – when the walls and trim are not prepared properly, the paint will highlight any imperfections. Loose paint and plaster need to be removed by scrapers or sandpaper. When covering previously painted trim, you should lightly sand the surface to create a key for the paint to bond to. You don't need to sand away all previous paint if the surface is in good condition.

4

Clean your entire working area to make sure it is completely free of dust and dirt.

5

Do not skip the priming or undercoating stage, however tempting that might be. Priming is designed to stabilize surfaces and prepare them for the paint. The primer coat may look patchy but it is not designed to conceal what it is covering, so don't worry.

6

Now comes the fun bit – the painting. Stir the paint in the tin for a few minutes to make sure it is mixed well and then decant it into your paint kettle and roller tray.

For further information about how to apply paint visit www.farrow-ball.com

7

Start with the ceiling. Brush in where the ceiling meets the wall, usually with a 50mm (2in) brush, taking care to apply the paint evenly. It's fine to come down onto the wall at this stage, as you will be painting over this with the wall colour.

Using the roller and pole, start rolling evenly across the ceiling area, overlapping by 50 per cent as you go. Start from your strongest source of light (usually a window) and work away from it until the ceiling is coated.

When the first coat is dry, repeat the process. Remember that you always need to apply two coats on each surface, so allow time for them to dry between coats.

8

Next, paint the walls. Cut* into the edge where the wall meets the ceiling without touching the finished ceiling colour. Some practice may be needed to get this line straight, so be patient.

Cut around all the wall edges, architraves and skirtings/baseboards – you can overlap with these areas slightly, as you will be painting over them with the relevant undercoat in the next step. Take care to apply the paint evenly as a thicker edge may show through the finished paint.

*Cutting-in / Cut in
Using a brush to paint areas a roller cannot
reach or where a neat edge is required.

9

Finally, paint the trim or woodwork. With your Interior Wood Primer & Undercoat and weapons of choice, usually a 25mm (1in) or 50mm (2in) brush, start to cut in the windows, doorframes, doors and finally the skirtings/baseboards making sure you don't go onto your finished walls. Once again, the edges may take some practice and patience to get your lines straight. Follow this with two topcoats. Always do your skirtings/baseboards last, as these are the areas that may pick up dust and so this avoids transferring it to other areas that are more noticeable.

10

When you have finished decorating, it is vital to keep a record of the colours and finishes you have used incase you need to touch up any areas in the future. Finally, be sure to store any leftover paint in a cool, dry place, protected from frost and extreme temperatures.

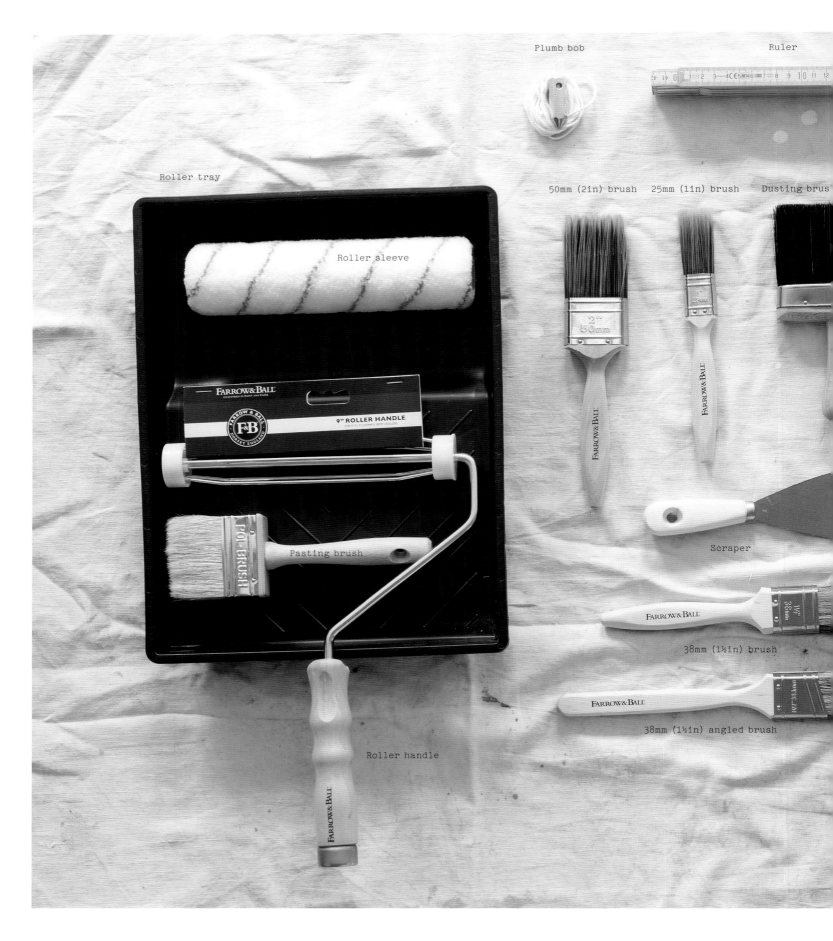

Plumb bob

Ruler

Roller tray

50mm (2in) brush   25mm (1in) brush   Dusting brush

Roller sleeve

Scraper

Pasting brush

38mm (1½in) brush

Roller handle

38mm (1½in) angled brush

Paper-hanging brush

Paint kettle

Masking
tape

Blades

Snap knife

Filling knife

Wallpaper scissors

Pasting brush

Tape measure

Decorator's sponge

Dust sheet

HOW LIGHT AFFECTS COLOUR

As we know, light is one of the most important things to take into consideration when choosing colours. The amount of natural light in a room and the direction that the room faces will have an enormous impact on a colour's appearance. The same colour can look different from room to room, at different times of the day and even in different seasons. This is what makes the colours so exciting and alive, but it may also add an extra complexity when you are choosing them.

The following is a brief summary of how light affects colours in rooms that face different directions.

NORTH-FACING ROOMS*

Although beloved by all artists for the clarity of the light, north-facing rooms do tend to make colours look cooler and harsher. As it can be difficult to create a sense of light and space in them, it may make sense not to fight nature. Instead, create dramatic, cocooning interiors by using strong colours like 'Brinjal', 'Vardo' or 'Inchyra Blue', which all create a sense of intimacy.

If you want lighter tones, avoid those that have a green or a grey base, and opt for yellow- or red-based colours instead, such as 'Ringwold Ground' or 'Tallow'. These will bounce any available light around the room.

SOUTH-FACING ROOMS*

Beautiful south-facing rooms are full of warm light for most of the day, and when the sun is out, everything appears more golden. To maximize this feeling of light and space, use pale tones. Soft blues like 'Pavilion Blue' or 'Cromarty' create a fresh look, while richer tones such as 'Joa's White' will create a warmer feel.

For a more contemporary edge, try colours with cool blue undertones, like 'Blackened' or 'Peignoir', and use 'All White' on the woodwork to give a crisp, fresh look.

EAST-FACING ROOMS*

The light in east-facing rooms is wonderfully bright in the morning, becoming more muted in the afternoon and evening. Colours sometimes look a little blue in eastern light, so it is best to work in harmony with cooler, light tones, choosing greens or blues. Warmer blues like 'Pale Powder' or 'Teresa's Green' work wonderfully, retaining some warmth in the evening but looking fresh in the morning.

*Applicable in the Northern Hemisphere.
The reverse is true in Southern climes.

FACING PAGE
This pretty, east-facing
Edinburgh bedroom is bathed
in early-morning sunlight.
'Pale Powder' on the walls
creates a warm and uplifting
atmosphere — the perfect
way to start the day.

THIS PAGE
'Strong White' has been used
on the walls of this south-
facing kitchen but in two
different finishes: Full Gloss
as a durable splashback, with
Modern Emulsion on the wall
above. The strong southern
light creates a stylish
contrast between the two
finishes for most of the day.

FACING PAGE

This west-facing room feels delightfully shady and cool for most of the day, but when the evening sun hits it, there is a welcome burst of light. 'Drop Cloth' painted on the walls and woodwork then becomes considerably warmer than it is in the morning.

BELOW

Small rooms lacking in natural light are always enhanced by the use of a dramatic colour. This internal bathroom looks fabulously opulent, with its walls painted in rich 'Charlotte's Locks', creating a jewel-like space that is a delight to enter.

WEST-FACING ROOMS

The light in west-facing rooms tends to be more muted in the morning and far more dramatic in the evening. Warm tones like 'Middleton Pink' or 'Smoked Trout' will accentuate the light in the afternoon and the evening sun. Greyer neutrals such as 'Slipper Satin' or 'Shadow White' will retain a feeling of light but will change from morning to evening – looking cooler earlier and warmer later.

WEST- AND EAST-FACING ROOMS

The light changes really dramatically throughout the day in these dual-aspect rooms. Count this as a blessing, as the colours on your walls will constantly surprise and thrill you. It is, however, often best to work out when you spend most of your time in these rooms and tailor your choice of colour to the type of light accordingly.

ARTIFICIAL LIGHT

As with natural light, artificial lighting also affects how colours can appear in a room. Halogen and incandescent bulbs emit a yellow light, making colours appear warmer, while LED bulbs give a blue light and are more suited to contemporary interiors. Bulbs that emit white light emulate daylight, which means that colours are rendered more accurately. When decorating a room that is often lit with candles, opt for velvety colours, such as 'Dead Salmon', or silvery colours, such as 'Ball Green', to give an intimate, romantic feel.

PART THREE

—

THE
DIRECTORY

FACING PAGE
The mesmerizing shape of
this beautiful winding
staircase means that very
little colour is needed on
the walls. Simple but warm
'Pointing' on both the walls
and woodwork complements
the aged wood perfectly.

COLOUR COMBINATIONS

———

The joy of the Farrow & Ball palette is that there are endless colour combinations at your fingertips. Of course, colours look quite different depending on the light conditions and where the colours are used, but the following combinations, chosen purely because they are my personal favourites, have been tried and tested in a huge range of properties worldwide. Each group creates wonderful spaces, whether subtle and understated or thrillingly dynamic. I hope there will be something here to appeal to everyone.

'Mahogany'
'Pink Ground'
'Setting Plaster'
'Tallow'

This group of colours creates tender, blushing rooms — perfect sanctuaries in our busy modern world. Use 'Pink Ground' on the walls, darker 'Setting Plaster' on the trim and 'Tallow', with its underlying warmth, on the ceiling. 'Mahogany' is the ideal accent colour to complement these delicate tones.

'Ammonite'
'Black Blue'
'Stiffkey Blue'
'Worsted'

This group is designed for those who want dark and moody interiors. 'Stiffkey Blue' is an intriguing alternative to charcoal and is particularly stylish when teamed with 'Worsted' on the woodwork. The ceiling should not be too white, so 'Ammonite', with its underlying grey tone, is ideal. Accents of 'Black Blue' serve to create even more drama.

'All White'
'Blue Ground'
'St Giles Blue'
'Yellowcake'

Although Farrow & Ball is famous for its sophisticated, muted palette, sometimes we crave cleaner colours. This surprising combination of uplifting 'St Giles Blue' on the walls with equally exciting 'Yellowcake' on the woodwork can't help but make you smile. 'Blue Ground' on the floor and 'All White' on the ceiling completes this lively scheme to perfection.

'Blue Gray'
'Cromarty'
'Pigeon'
'Shadow White'

This scheme always feels delightfully relaxed. Often used on exteriors, it is also a great favourite for informal kitchens, with 'Shadow White' on the walls, the mid-colour, 'Blue Gray', on any floor units to ground the scheme, lighter 'Cromarty' on the wall cupboards and the strongest colour, 'Pigeon', on the central island.

'Cabbage White'
'Drawing Room Blue'
'Lulworth Blue'
'Parma Gray'

For a breezy seaside feel, nothing beats 'Parma Gray' on the walls, with slightly darker 'Lulworth Blue' on the woodwork. Adding 'Drawing Room Blue' on the furniture or the floor introduces an interesting extra dimension, while 'Cabbage White' on the ceiling complements this cool blue scheme.

'Calke Green'
'Clunch'
'Eating Room Red'
'Print Room Yellow' (A)

These classic colours, each with roots in the past, are a sublime combination in a traditional setting. 'Eating Room Red', as the name suggests, is a big favourite for dining rooms, 'Print Room Yellow' (A) creates elegant drawing rooms, while 'Calke Green' is suitably dignified for a study. These three colours sit harmoniously together and work best with 'Clunch' on both the ceiling and the woodwork.

'Babouche'
'Blackened'
'Down Pipe'
'Railings'

Strong combinations such as this have become extremely popular. Both 'Babouche' and 'Railings' on the walls within a single space may at first feel a little daunting but because they have an equal weight of colour, they work fantastically together, creating really dynamic rooms. Slightly softer 'Down Pipe' looks wonderful on the woodwork, while 'Blackened' could be used on the floor.

'Oval Room Blue'
'Pointing'
'Print Room Yellow' (A)
'Yeabridge Green'

Although these colours are all sourced from traditional houses, they feel very modern when combined. If muted 'Oval Room Blue' is used in a hall, then rooms leading off it painted in 'Yeabridge Green' and 'Print Room Yellow' (A) are dynamic in contrast, especially when the colour features on both the walls and the woodwork. All the ceilings should be painted in uncomplicated 'Pointing'.

'Drop Cloth'
'French Gray'
'Shaded White'
'Shadow White'

Both 'Drop Cloth' and 'Shadow White' were created to work with the already existing 'Shaded White', the former being a darker shade than 'Shaded White' and the latter being slightly lighter. All three sit together seamlessly and can be used in any combination for a really understated beautiful scheme that is often enhanced by 'French Gray' on the furniture.

'Dove Tale'
'Great White'
'Peignoir'
'Pelt'

Although this combination was a favourite for classic boudoir bedrooms, in recent years it has burst out into sitting rooms, studies and even kitchens. Walls in dusty-looking 'Peignoir' are perfectly complemented by 'Dove Tale' woodwork, while intense 'Pelt' adds a dramatic twist. The underlying lilac tone of 'Great White' makes it ideal for the ceiling.

'Radicchio'
'Tanner's Brown'
'Vardo'
'Wimborne White'

This combination of colours was inspired directly by the intricate decoration of traditional Romany wagons — and it feels just as joyful in the home today. Strong 'Tanner's Brown' walls are the perfect backdrop to a kitchen dresser or bookcase painted in 'Vardo', with 'Radicchio' used on all the interior surfaces. 'Wimborne White' on the ceiling keeps things looking fresh.

'Inchyra Blue'
'Mole's Breath'
'Smoked Trout'
'Strong White'

Somehow, this mix of traditional and contemporary colours, which has long been a favourite combination of mine, sums up how we use Farrow & Ball colours today. Despite their reserved nature, 'Smoked Trout' on the walls and 'Inchyra Blue' on the woodwork never fail to thrill. With the addition of 'Mole's Breath' accents, something really magical happens. 'Strong White' is perfect on the ceiling.

221

USEFUL INFORMATION

Interior Finishes*	Use	Sheen	Colours available	Tin Size available**	Coverage m² per tin size***
Estate Emulsion	For interior walls and ceilings – our signature chalky matt finish	2%	132	100ml 2.5 litres 5 litres	1 35 70
Modern Emulsion	For interior walls and ceilings, including kitchens and bathrooms	7%	132	2.5 litres 5 litres	30 60
Estate Eggshell	For interior woodwork and metal, including radiators	20%	132	750ml 2.5 litres 5 litres	9 30 60
Floor Paint	For interior wood and concrete floors, including garages	40%	132	750ml 2.5 litres 5 litres	9 30 60
Full Gloss	For interior and exterior woodwork and metal	95%	132	750ml 2.5 litres	9 30

Exterior Finishes

Exterior Finishes	Use	Sheen	Colours available	Tin Size available**	Coverage m² per tin size***
Exterior Masonry	For exterior masonry surfaces	2%	107	5 litres	40
Exterior Eggshell	Durable finish for exterior wood and metal surfaces	20%	132	750ml 2.5 litres	10 32
Full Gloss	For interior and exterior woodwork and metal	95%	132	750ml 2.5 litres	9 30

Specialist Finishes

Specialist Finishes	Use	Sheen	Colours available	Tin Size available**	Coverage m² per tin size***
Casein Distemper	For interior plaster walls and ceilings	2%	131	2.5 litres 5 litres	32 65
Soft Distemper	For interior ceilings and fine plasterwork to enhance detailing	2%	63	5 litres	65
Limewash	For interior and exterior limestone, lime render and plaster	2%	79	5 litres	Varies on conditions
Dead Flat	For interior woodwork, plaster and metal	2%	132	750ml 2.5 litres 5 litres	9 30 60

* Not all finishes are available in all markets.

** For readers in the US requiring tin sizes in imperial units, please refer to www.farrow-ball.com

*** Coverage is dependent on thickness of application and surface type. Figures are based on one coat, although at least two coats are recommended.

THIS PAGE
I am constantly repainting the walls in my sitting room so that I can check the effect that the amazing light has on the colours. At this point — the colours have since changed — they were 'Dimpse', with 'Down Pipe' on the floor and 'All White' on the woodwork. This made a crisp but understated scheme: the perfect backdrop while I was writing this book, sitting at this very table.

A BRIEF HISTORY OF PAINT

From the countless archaeological discoveries made around the world, we know that colour was used for cave painting 40,000 years ago. Early man extracted pigments from the earth or charcoal and mixed them with saliva, to create a very early form of paint. It is thrilling to know that humans have felt the need to enhance their surroundings with colour since prehistory.

Over the years, pigments used for making paints have been derived from a number of different sources, such as minerals, elements, plants, vegetables and even insects. The medium, the liquid element, could be a variety of substances, from oil to egg yolk.

The residents of Pompeii were early exponents of interior design and used colour on the walls of their homes to display their wealth. At certain times in history some pigments were as precious as gold, particularly ultramarine, made from lapis lazuli, which was first seen in the architectural wonders of Ancient Egypt.

During the 17th century, paint makers and house painters would grind a mixture of pigment and oil into a paste with a mortar and pestle. Sadly, this process, which was done by hand, exposed them to lead poisoning because of the inclusion of white-lead powder.

The 19th century brought industrialization, and the advances in chemistry led to many inventions that changed the world of colour completely, particularly machines that ground pigments. Paint could now be manufactured by suspending pigments in inexpensive linseed oil, which kept it from drying too quickly. Suddenly colour was within everyone's reach and new colours abounded – cadmium, cobalt, viridian and cerulean all brought new-found joy into homes. Interior house painting, both for decorative reasons and to protect walls from damp, increasingly became the norm as the 19th century progressed.

As a result of World War II, there was a shortage of linseed oil, and paint makers turned to easier-to-make artificial resins that held colour brilliantly, as well as creating long-lasting paint.

In the late 20th century, lead-based paints were banned for use in residential homes. As the environmental movement grew over the next 30 years, Farrow & Ball led the market by making only water-based paints with low or minimal VOCs (Volatile Organic Compounds – the nasty bits in paint; also see page 228).

Luckily, man has always felt the need to capture the vibrant world around him, which is why we have the fantastic evolution of colour and paint as we know it today.

THE FARROW & BALL DIFFERENCE

What makes Farrow & Ball different? We can all see something very special when a room has been decorated in our paint – there is a certain depth of colour and sophistication – but why is that?

Well, at Farrow & Ball we believe in never compromising on quality. We still go to great lengths to use only the finest ingredients in our paint and the pigments that go into them are unmatched in their richness. In addition, we take great care to pack our paint with pigment rather than cheap plastic fillers.

Farrow & Ball paints also offer exceptional performance in all finishes, as well as being low-odour and eco-friendly, so they are safe and easy to use throughout every home. And our thoughtfully created palette of 132 timeless colours makes it easy to design colour schemes that work in seamless harmony, whether in a modern or traditional house.

We are very proud of our paint and wallpaper (see page 250), which is also made with unsurpassed care and expertise. It all sounds simple, and in many ways it is. We just use the finest ingredients and high quantities of pigment, which results in incomparable colours and finishes.

Pigment

Water

Extender

Resin

Additives

ENVIRONMENTAL INFORMATION

The enivronment is very important to us at Farrow & Ball and we do as much as we can to help protect it. Although we know we're not perfect, the more we do, the better we get. From the creation of our water-based paints and our wallpapers that are printed onto paper sourced from FSC® (Forest Stewardship Council) accredited suppliers to raw materials, energy use, packaging and distribution, we are motivated by a desire to care for our environment.

Our water-based paints contain low or minimal VOCs (Volatile Organic Compounds). In paints, VOCs tend to be solvents, such as white spirit, which evaporate as paint dries, releasing pollutants into the atmosphere. A water-based paint is kinder to the environment, and its low odour is great for your home as well. Our paints have been independently tested and approved, so parents can rest assured when decorating their children's nurseries and bedrooms, or painting children's accessories, toys or cots.

As all our paints are water-based, brushes and rollers can be washed out with warm, soapy water after use, eliminating the need to use any polluting white spirit solutions.

At Farrow & Ball we are doing everything we can to prove that beauty doesn't have to cost the earth.

FACING PAGE

Chic 'Railings' has been used on the exterior doors of the inner courtyard of this Paris house, to echo the colour of the glazed interior doors. A magical colour, 'Railings' is difficult to pin down — it always looks more blue when viewed on larger surfaces.

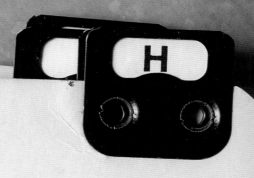

PAINT FINISHES

Don't be overwhelmed by the choice of different paint finishes. Unless you are doing specialist decorating, there is really only a choice of two for the walls: the very flat matt Estate Emulsion or the equally beautiful but more durable Modern Emulsion. Similarly, there is a choice of two finishes for woodwork: the flatter Estate Eggshell or the high sheen Full Gloss.

Whichever finish you choose, you are safe in the knowledge that our interior and exterior paint finishes are water-based, low-odour, quick-drying, environmentally friendly and child-friendly.

Interior Finishes Estate Emulsion, Modern Emulsion, Estate Eggshell, Floor Paint, Full Gloss. Traditional and specialist finishes: Dead Flat, Limewash, Soft Distemper, Casein Distemper.

Exterior Finishes Exterior Masonry, Exterior Eggshell, Full Gloss. Traditional and specialist finishes: Limewash.

Primers and Undercoats Wall & Ceiling Primer & Undercoat, Wood Floor Primer & Undercoat, Wood Knot & Resin Blocking Primer, Metal Primer & Undercoat, Masonry & Plaster Stabilising Primer, Exterior Wood Primer & Undercoat.

Note that not all finishes are available in all markets.

The true nature of Estate Emulsion is perfectly demonstrated here. The 'Stiffkey Blue' walls look so rich that you want to stroke them, especially when they are contrasted with 'All White' Estate Eggshell.

Estate Emulsion has only a 2 per cent sheen level, which not only gives it enormous depth, but also means that the colour changes according to the light. 'Buff' (A) looks beautiful here in the morning light.

'Shaded White' Estate Emulsion feels delightfully relaxed in this eclectic living room. The exceptional depth of colour is clearly evident in even the most neutral of schemes, particularly when it is contrasted, as here, with 'Wimborne White' Estate Eggshell on the woodwork.

ESTATE EMULSION

This paint finish is responsible for the coveted signature look of Farrow & Ball. Suitable for use on walls as well as ceilings, it has a chalky, very flat matt finish and an unmatched depth of colour.

MODERN EMULSION

Modern Emulsion is the ultimate high-performance alternative to Estate Emulsion. It is washable, as well as stain- and scuff-resistant, but retains the Farrow & Ball signature flat matt finish and depth of colour. Being both tough and beautiful makes it ideal for walls and ceilings throughout the home, and it is particularly recommended for children's bedrooms, high-traffic hallways and high-moisture areas such as kitchens and bathrooms.

FACING PAGE
'All White' Modern Emulsion is the perfect colour and finish for the walls of this busy Dutch kitchen, where it not only has to withstand family life but also burgeoning foliage. Its 7 per cent sheen level helps to bounce all the light flooding in through the magnificent window around this huge space.

ABOVE LEFT
Halls and stairs are particularly susceptible to grubby fingers and knocks and bangs from bags. In this London hall, Modern Emulsion in 'Blue Gray' provides extra protection and any marks can be easily removed.

ABOVE RIGHT
'Off-Black' Modern Emulsion is a brave but stylish choice for this small bathroom. The colour looks chic and the durability of the finish is perfect for withstanding the steamy conditions.

BELOW LEFT
The wooden interior of
photographer James Merrell's
houseboat has been painted
in 'Purbeck Stone' Estate
Eggshell — durable as well as
very stylish. The mid-sheen
level also helps to reflect
any light off the ceiling.

BELOW RIGHT
The 'Parma Gray' of this
short corridor wall contrasts
with the other neutral walls
and makes the space feel more
square. The door has been
painted the same colour, but
in Estate Eggshell, to create
a seamless feel.

FACING PAGE
Fabulous 'Porphyry Pink' (A)
Estate Eggshell has been
used on these closets that
span an entire wall in a
bedroom where the remaining
walls are the same colour,
but Estate Emulsion. Had
the closets been painted the

white of the woodwork, the
proportions of the room would
have been ruined and the
space would feel much smaller.

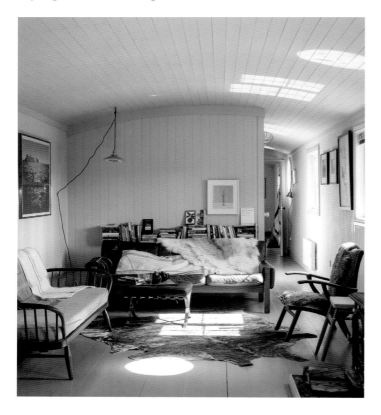

ESTATE EGGSHELL

Despite its fragile namesake, Estate Eggshell is an extremely
robust and durable eggshell finish that is easily washed and
wiped clean, making it ideal for interior woodwork and metal,
including radiators. Its mid-sheen appearance means it is the ideal
complement to Estate Emulsion and Modern Emulsion.

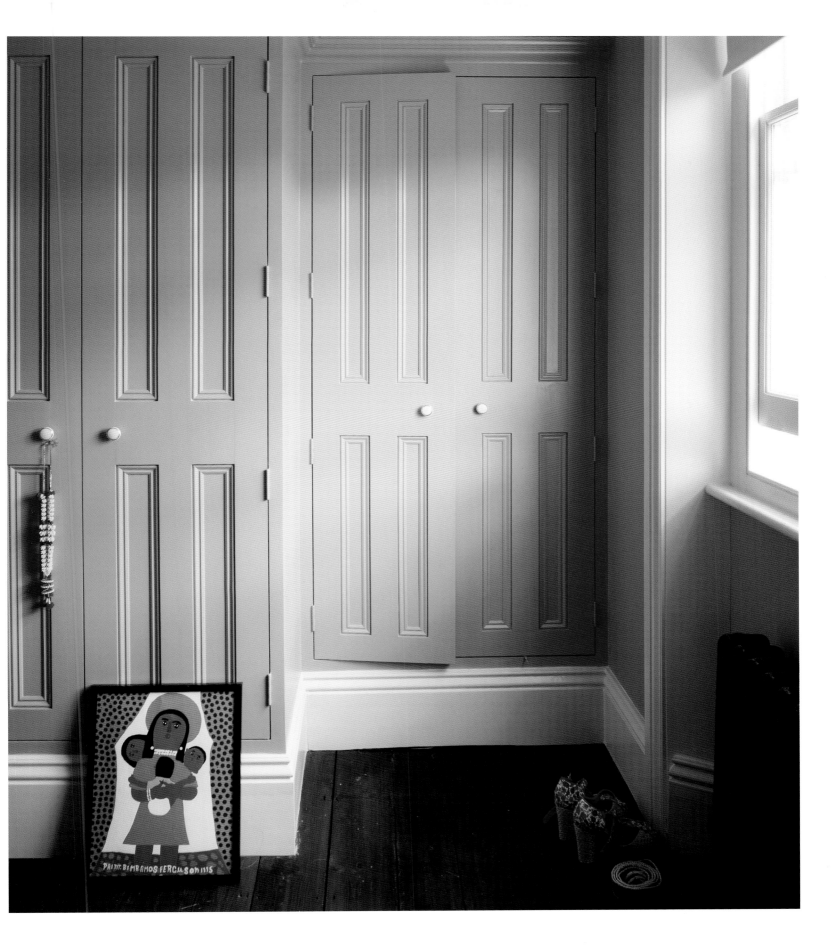

FULL GLOSS

This traditional high-gloss finish is extremely versatile and robust, and is suitable for both interior and exterior use. Although more usually reserved for woodwork, current trends see it being used on both walls and ceilings, to provide a little glamour.

FACING PAGE
To add an extra dimension to this stylish room, 'Railings' Full Gloss has been used on the woodwork, an effective contrast to the flat 'Cinder Rose' walls. The Full Gloss bounces the light off the shutters and creates a traditional feel.

THIS PAGE
A bespoke green gloss paint was made for the front door of this Scottish croft, creating a dramatic entrance that contrasts with the 'Chinese Blue' (A) and 'Old White' of the porch. Full Gloss is the perfect durable finish for extreme weather conditions.

BELOW LEFT

'Light Gray' Dead Flat looks
magnificent on the walls of
this bedroom. The depth of
colour is unsurpassed and
the finish is invitingly flat
and chalky.

BELOW RIGHT

The use of 'Claydon Blue' (A)
in this study is the perfect
choice to complement the
simple but dramatic rug.
The Dead Flat finish on the
walls gives extra depth to
this pared-down space.

FACING PAGE

A strong colour such as
'Railings', which is more
blue than black, looks
particularly stunning when
used in the Dead Flat finish.
Although a traditional
finish, it is still popular
with discerning decorators
who wish to create rich
interiors, as seen in this
house in Holland.

DEAD FLAT

This traditional, completely flat matt finish can be used on a
variety of surfaces – interior woodwork, plaster and metal – where
an exceptionally matt and elegant finish is required. It is, though,
unsuitable for use in kitchens or bathrooms, on furniture or areas
of heavy wear because it is inclined to mark.

FACING PAGE
Painted in 'Shaded White'
Floor Paint, these glossy
stairs not only bounce
light around the hall,
but also create a dramatic
contrast to the 'Railings'
walls, while maintaining a
certain relaxed atmosphere.

BELOW
'Down Pipe', the colour
of the walls and woodwork
in the adjacent hall, has
been used on the floor of this
particularly friendly London
sitting room. This links
the two spaces together and
makes the room feel wider.

FLOOR PAINT

This hard-wearing paint has a mid-sheen/semi-gloss finish, which will bring any interior wood or concrete floor to life. It can also be used as an alternative to Estate Eggshell and Full Gloss on furniture and kitchen cupboards, as well as skirtings/baseboards and other trim. It is, however, unsuitable for decking or any other exposed exterior floor.

EXTERIOR EGGSHELL

This mid-sheen finish is suitable for use on exterior wood and metal, including softwood and hardwood window frames, cladding and garden furniture. The paint is durable, flexible and highly resistant to flaking, peeling and fading for up to six years. It is fungi- and water-resistant, and at the same time breathable, to help minimize wood rot. It can also be used on railings, gates, guttering and other metal surfaces.

EXTERIOR MASONRY

This high-performance finish, designed for use on masonry surfaces, has the very flat matt apperance that is the hallmark of Farrow & Ball paint, while being extremely tough, hard-wearing and exceptionally durable. The breathable, fungi- and water-resistant formula helps to combat damp in walls, and is resistant to peeling, cracking, chalking, blistering and fading for up to 15 years.

RIGHT
The combination of 'Joa's White' Exterior Masonry on the walls and 'Stone Blue' Full Gloss on the bench makes for an irresistible spot in which to shelter in the garden of this beautiful Dorset cottage.

FACING PAGE
The traditional use of 'All White' Exterior Masonry on this British seaside house may be too austere for some. However, when complemented by the 'Yellowcake' Exterior Eggshell door, it cannot fail to make you smile.

SPECIALIST FINISHES

For the sympathetic decorating of historic and traditional properties, our specialist finishes are the essential ingredients for creating an authentic look:

CASEIN DISTEMPER

This strengthened distemper has added casein, which is produced from milk protein and has been used as an ingredient in paint since the ancient Egyptian times. Suitable for interior plastered walls and ceilings, it has excellent coverage, breathes well and achieves a superb flat finish – perfect for specialist decorators in older homes.

SOFT DISTEMPER

This simple, traditional distemper is bound with natural resins to create a very flat and exquisitely powdery finish. It is perfect for repainting intricate ceilings and plasterwork, as its soft nature allows easy removal, therefore maintaining fine details.

LIMEWASH

Creating a highly traditional look, this ready-to-use Limewash is suitable for interior walls and ceilings, as well as external walls. Limewash works by bonding itself to the underlying layer, becoming part of the building itself, often creating an aged, mottled finish. Available in white and selected colours, Limewash should only be used by specialist decorators; please refer to our website or colour card for details.

PRIMERS & UNDERCOATS

Remember that preparation is key to successful decoration. To make certain that you have the most beautiful and long-lasting interiors, each of our 132 colours has a recommended Primer & Undercoat colour, which has been created to ensure you have a surface primed for attention in order to achieve a fortified finish. These Primers & Undercoats are formulated with the same ingredients and rich pigments that enhance our topcoats.

WALL & CEILING PRIMER & UNDERCOAT

Designed for use under Estate Emulsion and Modern Emulsion, this Primer & Undercoat will achieve an even finish for the topcoat.

INTERIOR WOOD PRIMER & UNDERCOAT

For use on bare wood or previously painted wood surfaces. This product will help you to achieve a perfect base on which to apply your chosen finish.

EXTERIOR WOOD PRIMER & UNDERCOAT

For use on exterior woodwork, to provide a protective, flexible and breathable foundation.

METAL PRIMER & UNDERCOAT

A rust-inhibiting Primer & Undercoat for metal surfaces, including metal gates, railings, furniture, radiators and downpipes.

MASONRY & PLASTER STABILISING PRIMER

For use on interior and exterior masonry, rendered or plastered surfaces that are porous, chalky or slightly degraded but otherwise structurally sound.

WOOD KNOT & RESIN BLOCKING PRIMER

For use on interior and exterior woodwork. This Primer blocks resinous stains on bare hardwoods, resinous softwoods and knotty areas. It should also be used as a patch primer on wooden floors before applying Wood Floor Primer & Undercoat.

WOOD FLOOR PRIMER & UNDERCOAT

For use on interior wood before applying Floor Paint. This will give the best foundation and a longer-lasting finish.

ABOVE
A 'Charlotte's Locks' feature wall in this sewing room makes an exciting backdrop for all dress designs.

FACING PAGE
'Blue Gray' on the walls of this hall creates a calming central hub in a busy family home.

WALLPAPERS

Although most wallpapers are made using ink, ours are not. We use our own paint to create the print, as well as the background colour, using traditional block or trough methods. This results in totally unique papers that work perfectly with the paint colours.

Our huge range of designs are inspired by archives of fabrics and wallpapers from around the world. There are florals, damasks, stripes and geometric patterns, some of which are large and flamboyant, while others are quietly subtle. Hopefully, there is something to appeal to everyone.

In order to make these wallpapers appropriate for use in the modern-day home, endless work has gone into ensuring that they are washable while still having the same chalky finish that has always defined the paint colours – a combination of timeless artistry and 21st-century durability.

BELOW LEFT
This charming 'Jasmine'
(BP 3905) wallpaper has a
'Green Smoke' background,
while the pattern is in
'Cooking Apple Green'.
Here, it is shown as a
gilt-framed panel against
a 'Dix Blue' wall.

BELOW RIGHT
Beautiful 'Lotus' (BP 2011)
wallpaper always causes a
stir, especially in this
brave colourway. The pattern
is in 'Charleston Gray',
which also features on the
woodwork. The background
is 'Wimborne White'.

FLORALS

Sumptuous 'Peony', 'Wisteria' and 'Versailles' are large, blowsy patterns often favoured for feature walls, as are the more contemporary 'Bamboo', 'Ringwold' and 'Rosslyn'. With their touch of the botanical, these are wonderful for creating pretty, traditional spaces, just like the smaller 'Uppark' and 'Jasmine', both of which can also be taken onto the ceilings. 'Feuille' has the simplicity of an original woodblock, so is perfect for those wanting a mid-century feel. In its netural and pastel tones, delicate 'Samphire' appeals to more traditional tastes, but it is certainly more on trend in the copper and grey colourways.

DAMASKS

Farrow & Ball have always been famous for their damasks. The smaller patterns of 'Brocade' and 'Renaissance' are perfect when combined with either their background or pattern colour – usually the paint below the dado rail and the paper above. The larger damasks, like the stunningly pretty French 'St Antoine' and its simpler English counterpart 'Silvergate', along with the more graphic 'Orangerie', appear very traditional when used in strong colours, but in contemporary houses decorated in more neutral combinations, the pattern becomes subtler. This is also true of the modern-looking 'Lotus', although the strong colourways are extremely popular with those looking to make a grand statement.

BELOW LEFT
'Tessella' (BP 3605) wallpaper
always feels confident and
poised, but in this colourway
it is also fresh and
uplifting. The background
is 'Blue Ground', while the
pattern is simple 'All White'.

BELOW RIGHT
'Chromatic Stripe' (BP 4201)
wallpaper never fails to
look chic. Here, the clean
colourway, made up from
the Architectural Neutrals,
works perfectly teamed with
the 'Pavilion Gray' woodwork.

GEOMETRIC

Most Farrow & Ball geometric papers tend to break up the wall, preventing it from feeling too flat, rather than creating a pattern. 'Tourbillon' and 'Vermicelli' are both excellent at doing this, while the diminutive patterns in 'Polka Square', 'Renaissance Leaves' and 'Yukutori' almost disappear at a distance but bring hidden delights close-up. The traditional 'Crivelli Trellis' is perfect for the country bedroom, while bold 'Tessella' is a firm favourite for garden rooms. These are complemented by the subtler 'Lattice' and 'Amime', both of which can be hung vertically or horizontally, as can 'Parquet'. 'Brockhampton Star' is the prettiest and most traditional of papers and can be used on both walls and ceilings, while the equally traditional 'Bumble Bee' just makes you smile.

STRIPES

Farrow & Ball stripes come in many shapes and sizes and are enduringly popular. They are, however, all timelessly elegant, from the classic one-colour 'Plain Stripe' and its wider version 'Broad Stripe' to the more graphic 'Chromatic Stripe', which includes four colours. For those who want a little more pattern in their stripes, 'Tented Stripe' and 'Block Print Stripe' offer an extra twist and work as well in children's rooms as they do in traditional studies. Because of their neutral backgrounds, 'Closet Stripe' and 'Five Over Stripe' are perfect for those craving a fresh, uncomplicated feel. All stripes can be hung vertically, in the more traditional way, or horizontally, to create more unusual spaces. However they are used, our stripes always appear to be smart and classic.

ARCHIVE

A t Farrow & Ball, we have always believed in keeping an easy-to-use palette. Although we have created many new colours, our colour card has never featured any more than the 132 colours we feel will most appeal to the current market. So when new colours are developed, it is with a heavy heart that we have to retire some still much-loved paint shades from the chart. 'Fake Tan', 'Monkey Puzzle', 'Pea Green' and 'Biscuit' are just a few of the archived but still greatly treasured Farrow & Ball colours. Never fear that they are not still readily available, and in any finish. Despite the fact that they may not be stocked in our showrooms, they can easily be ordered from the factory, where the original recipes are kept safely in our archives. Many old favourites have been subtly changed to suit the contemporary home and come back as new colours, but if you still love a colour, be it 'Single Cream' or 'Fruit Fool', they are only a phone call away. All archive colours in this book have been marked '(A)'.

FACING PAGE
Our original and treasured paint chart and our archive colour fan, to where much-loved colours are retired.

OVERLEAF
The use of calming 'Blackened' on the walls of this eclectic kitchen capitalizes on the enormous amount of natural light. The units painted in 'Railings' ground the space and tie in with the frames of the bifold doors.

Farrow & Ball Ltd

Paints Develo...

...ional Trust

BRAG

WHITE

8 STRING
U/C 1

15 BONE
U/C 1

22 LIGHT BLUE
U/C 22

27 PARM
U/C 2

U/C 1

9 LIGHT STONE
U/C 15

16 CORD
U/C 15

23 POWDER BLUE
U/C 22

28

51 SUDBURY YELLOW U/C 37

10 FAWN
U/C 15

17 LIGHT GRAY
U/C 10

24 BALLROOM BLUE
U/C 22

STONE WHITE
U/C 15

18 FRENCH GRAY
U/C 32

52 STRAW
U/C 37

EEN ONE
U/C 18

19 LICHEN
U/C 18

25 PIGEON
U/C 22

53 CANE
U/C 37

26 DOV

54 DAUPHIN
U/C 18

20 BUFF
U/C 10

OIL U...
Nos. 1, 10,...

DEAD FLAT OIL...

OIL EGGSHELL is available in W...

55 WAINSCOT
U/C 49

OIL FULL GLOSS is available in W...

ESTATE EMULSION is available in White and all 57 colo...

21 OINTMENT PINK
U/C 10

OIL BOUND DISTEMPER is available in White and
Nos. 1, 2, 3, 4, 8, 15, 16, 21, 22, 23, 27, 29, 32, 37, 44, 50, 51.
SOFT DISTEMPER is available in White and
Nos. 1, 3, 4, 8, 15,

U/C 49

56 ETRUSCAN RED
U/C 49

EXTERIOR MASONRY PAINT is available in
Nos. 1, 3, 4, 6, 9, 15, 21, 37, 44.

43 EATING ROOM RED
U/C 49

50 BOOK ROOM RED
U/C 49

57 OFF-BLACK
U/C 26

We reserve the right at any time to amend any of the above colours.

F&B
FARROW & BALL
DORSET ENGLAND

ARCHIVE
COLOURS

FARROW & BALL

GLOSSARY

Architrave
Moulding around a door or window.

Ceiling rose
Rounded decoration, usually mounted on the centre of the ceiling.

Cornice/crown moulding
A decorative border where the wall meets the ceiling.

Coving
A simple concave border used to eliminate the interior angle between the wall and ceiling.

Dado
The lower part of the wall below the dado/chair rail when decorated differently from the wall above it.

Dado rail/chair rail
A horizontal moulding fixed to an interior wall at around waist height.

Fanlight
A window over a door.

Frieze
The upper part of the wall between the picture rail and the cornice. Or an ornamental band around the top of the wall.

Panelling
Wood or plaster panels lining a wall.

Picture rail
A horizontal moulding fixed to an interior wall from which pictures can be hung.

Skirting/baseboard
A border of wood (or occasionally plaster) that is joined to the bottom of an interior wall where it meets the floor to protect it from kicks and dirt.

Tongue and groove/ bead board
Boards fitted edge to edge to create panelling.

Wainscoting
Wood panelling covering the lower part of the wall.

Woodwork/trim
A blanket term for skirting/ baseboard, doors and frames, windows and frames, and any additional joinery.

FARROW & BALL SHOWROOMS

UK

Bath
124–6 Walcot Street
Bath
Somerset
BA1 5BG
+44 (0) 1225 466700

Battersea
146 Northcote Road
Battersea
London
SW11 6RD
+44 (0) 20 7228 6578

Beaconsfield
39 London End
Old Beaconsfield
Buckinghamshire
HP9 2HW
+44 (0) 1494 677700

Blackheath
48 Tranquil Vale
Blackheath
London
SE3 0BD
+44 (0) 20 8318 4897

Bristol
19 Princess Victoria Street
Clifton
Bristol
BS8 4BP
+44 (0) 1179 733900

Cambridge
14 Regent Street
Cambridge
Cambridgeshire
CB2 1DB
+44 (0) 1223 367771

Chelsea
249 Fulham Road
Chelsea
London
SW3 6HY
+44 (0) 20 7351 0273

Edinburgh
20 North West Circus Place
Stockbridge
Edinburgh
West Lothian
EH3 6SX
+44 (0) 131 226 2216

Esher
15 High Stree
Esher
Surrey
KT10 9RL
+44 (0) 1372 477129

Glasgow
470 Great Western Road
Glasgow
G12 8EW
+44 (0) 141 337 7043

Guildford
11 Tunsgate
Guildford
Surrey
GU1 3QT
+44 (0) 1483 511365

Hampstead
58 Rosslyn Hill
Hampstead
London
NW3 1ND
+44 (0) 20 7435 5169

Harrogate
1 James Street
Harrogate
North Yorkshire
HG1 1QS
+44 (0) 1423 522 552

Henley-on-Thames
21 Thameside
Henley-on-Thames
Oxfordshire
RG9 2LJ
+44 (0) 1491 636128

Hove
31b Western Road
Hove
East Sussex
BN3 1AF
+44 (0) 1273 774640

Islington
38 Cross Street
Islington
London
N1 2BG
+44 (0) 20 7226 2627

Leamington Spa
82 Regent Street
Leamington Spa
Warwickshire
CV32 4NS
+44 (0) 1926 424760

Manchester
270 Deansgate
Manchester
M3 4JB
+44 (0) 161 839 5532

Marylebone
64 Paddington Street
Marylebone
London
W1U 4JG
+44 (0) 20 7487 4733

Notting Hill
21–22 Chepstow Corner
Notting Hill
London
W2 4XE
+44 (0) 20 7221 2328

Oxford
225 Banbury Road
Summertown
Oxford
OX2 7HS
+44 (0) 1865 559575

Richmond
30 Hill Rise
Richmond
Surrey
TW10 6UA
+44 (0) 20 8948 7700

Solihull
36 Mill Lane
Mell Square Shopping Centre
Solihull
West Midlands
B91 3BA
+44 (0) 121 709 3360

St Albans
36 Market Place
St Albans
Hertfordshire
AL3 5DG
+44 (0) 1727 847155

Sunningdale
5 Broomhall Buildings
Sunningdale
Surrey
SL5 0DH
+44 (0) 1344 876615

Tunbridge Wells
4 High Street
Tunbridge Wells
Kent
TN1 1UX
+44 (0) 1892 512121

Wilmslow
19 Church Street
Wilmslow
Cheshire
SK9 1AX
+44 (0) 1625 415102

Wimbledon
90 High Street
Wimbledon
London
SW19 5EG
+44 (0) 20 8605 2099

Wimborne
Uddens Estate
Wimborne
Dorset
BH21 7NL
+44 (0) 1202 890905

Winchester
32 The Square
Winchester
Hampshire
SO23 9EX
+44 (0) 1962 843179

EUROPE

Dublin
14 Cornmarket
Dublin 8
IRELAND
+353 1 67 70 111

Düsseldorf
Hohe Straße 37
40213 Düsseldorf
GERMANY
+49 21 12 10 73 561

Frankfurt
Kaiserstraße 25
60311 Frankfurt
GERMANY
+49 69 24 24 62 69

Hamburg
Neue ABC-Strraße. 2–3
20354
Hamburg
GERMANY

Paris Rive Gauche
50 rue de l'université
75007 Paris
FRANCE
+33 1 45 44 82 20

Paris Marais
111 bis, rue de Turenne
75003 Paris
FRANCE
+33 1 44 61 18 22

Paris Neuilly
2 rue du Chateau
Neuilly - sur - Seine
92200 Paris
FRANCE
+33 1 47 22 98 28

Paris St Germain en Laye
7 Rue du Docteur Timsit
St Germain En Laye
78100 Paris
FRANCE
+33 1 39 10 46 50

Munich
Rumfordstraße 48
80469 Munich
GERMANY
+49 89 21 26 94 16

Strasbourg
1 Rue de la Nuee Bleue
67000 Strasbourg
FRANCE
+33 390 20 08 40

NORTH AMERICA

Boston
One Design Center Place
Suite 337A
Boston
MA 02210
USA
+1 617 345 5344

Chicago
449 North Wells Street
Chicago
IL 60654
USA

Greenwich
32 East Putnam Avenue
Greenwich
CT 06830
USA
+1 203 422 0990

Los Angeles
8475 Melrose Avenue
West Hollywood
Los Angeles
CA 90069
USA
+1 323 655 4499

NY Flatiron
32 East 22nd Street
New York
NY 10010
USA
+1 212 334 8330

NY Midtown
D&D Building Suite 1519
979 Third Avenue
New York
NY 10022
USA
+1 212 752 5544

NY Upper East Side
142 East 73rd Street
New York
NY 10021
USA
+1 212 737 7400

NY Upper West Side
322 Columbus Avenue
New York
NY 10023
USA
+1 212 799 0900

Orange County
3323 Suite C Hyland Avenue
Costa Mesa
CA 92626
USA
+1 714 438 2448

Toronto
1054 Yonge Street
Toronto
ON M4W 2L1
CANADA
+1 416 920 0200

Washington
5221 Wisconsin Avenue NW
Washington DC
DC 20015
USA
+1 202 479 6780

Westport
396 Post Rd East
Westport
CT 06880
USA
+1 203 221 3117

For the most up-to-date list
of showrooms and
stockists please visit
www.farrow-ball.com

INDEX

—

ACKNOWLEDGEMENTS

Many thanks go to all at Octopus who expertly nursed this first time writer through the process of creating a book, particularly to Alison Starling for her unfailing support and advice, to Jonathan Christie for his thoughtful design, and Polly Poulter for her extraordinary diligence.

We are obviously indebted to the home owners from all over the world who so generously allowed us to photograph their beautiful properties and include them in this book.

James Merrell's brilliant photographs have made this book what it is, so we owe him untold appreciation, not only for his fabulous images, but also for his willingness to travel the world at the drop of a hat.

Special thanks to the wonderfully talented Farrow & Ball team – too great in number to mention by name, although the hard work and commitment of Shamus Pitts (colour wheel supremo), Bel Moretti, Jo Tucker and Tracey Mack deserve particular gratitude.

The extraordinary generosity and hard work of Lawrence Showell and Jonathan Bear deserves particular thanks as well.

Cosmo Studholme should certainly be mentioned for his unfailing patience in both proof reading his mother's words and dealing with the occasional technical breakdown!

Importantly, I would like to thank my colleague and friend Charlie for making the process of creating this book such fun.

And lastly my biggest thanks go to A., C. & N. for always being there.

— *Joa Studholme*

An Hachette UK Company
www.hachette.co.uk

First published in Great Britain in 2016 by
Mitchell Beazley,
a division of Octopus Publishing Group Ltd,
Carmelite House,
50 Victoria Embankment,
London EC4Y 0DZ
www.octopusbooks.co.uk
www.octopusbooksusa.com

Text and illustrations
copyright © Farrow & Ball Limited 2016

Distributed in the US by Hachette Book Group,
1290 Avenue of the Americas,
4th and 5th Floors,
New York, NY 10020

Distributed in Canada by
Canadian Manda Group
664 Annette St., Toronto, Ontario,
Canada M6S 2C8

ISBN 978-1-78472-087-2

A CIP catalogue record for this book is available
from the British Library.

Printed and bound in China

10 9 8 7 6 5 4 3 2 1

Text: Joa Studholme
Photographers: James Merrell, Robin Kitchin,
James Bowden and Justin Barton

Publisher: Alison Starling
Creative Director: Jonathan Christie
Editor: Pollyanna Poulter
Copy Editor: Helen Ridge
Proofreader: Zia Mattocks
Senior Production Manager: Katherine Hockley

JOA STUDHOLME

Having joined Farrow & Ball over 19 years ago, Joa Studholme has amassed a vast wealth of experience. From developing the new colours to consulting on design projects, Joa has worked with the paints and papers every day on both residential and commercial projects. A self-confessed 'colour geek', Joa's passion for interior design and colour means her own home is under constant renovation and she claims to redecorate it at least once a month.

CHARLOTTE COSBY

Head of Creative, Charlotte Cosby, has been working with Farrow & Ball for the past nine years. She has full responsibility for creative direction, including product development, brand identity, photography, showroom design and much more. Charlotte is passionate about pattern, colour and design and spends much of her free time redecorating her Victorian apartment by the sea.

JAMES MERRELL

London-based James Merrell is the book's photographer. James's work has been featured in *W*, *Elle Decor* (all editions), *Vogue Living*, *Town & Country*, *Domino*, *Food & Wine*, *Martha Stewart Living*, *Departures*, *Travel + Leisure*, *The Wall Street Journal* and *Living Etc*. It has also appeared in many bestselling interiors books.